READING-LITERATURE
TEACHER'S GUIDE

To accompany *The Primer* and
First and *Second Reader*

BY

HARRIETTE TAYLOR TREADWELL
PRINCIPAL, WEST PULLMAN SCHOOL, CHICAGO

AND

MARGARET FREE
PRIMARY TEACHER, FORESTVILLE SCHOOL, CHICAGO, 1898-1908

LIVING BOOKS PRESS EDITION
EDITED BY
SHEILA CARROLL
AND
BOBBIE DAILEY

LIVING BOOKS PRESS
MOUNT PLEASANT, MICHIGAN

READING-LITERATURE TEACHER'S GUIDE: TO ACCOMPANY THE PRIMER AND FIRST AND SECOND READER is an unabridged edition of an original work published in 1916 as PRIMARY READING AND LITERATURE, A MANUAL FOR TEACHERS: TO ACCOMPANY THE PRIMER, FIRST AND SECOND READERS, by Row, Peterson & Co. Living Books Press™ has edited the original text to improve readability, accuracy, and useability.

LIVING BOOKS PRESS™

Publishers of classic living books

5497 Gilmore Road

Mt. Pleasant, Michigan 48858

www.livingbookscurriculum.com

ISBN-13: 978-1-938192-01-2

v.07.16

Design and prepress by

Carrousel Graphics, Jackson, Wyoming

Printed in the United States of America

Living Books Press is the publishing company of Living Books Curriculum, a complete K-8 Christian homeschooling solution based on the visionary philosophy of pioneering educator Charlotte Mason. To learn more, visit our website: www.livingbookscurriculum.com.

CONTENTS

OTHER SOURCES OF THE STORIES AND POEMS

THE FOLK TALES OF *SECOND READER*

LIVING BOOKS PRESS EDITION PREFACE

The debate about the best way to teach reading has been going on for over two centuries. The discussion revolves around two different ways to teach—by the look of the word or the sound of its letters. Other terms used to describe this process are look-and-say vs. letter sounds or sight words vs. phonics. These two approaches form the basis for all reading instruction.

The phonetic method

Teaching reading with the phonetic method (letter sounds) became well-known in the United States shortly after the American Revolution. Noah Webster, creator of the first American dictionary, felt British primers and readers were not consistent with language and usage of the new republic, and so he created his own reading approach, referred to as the "speller." In 1783, he published his first "speller" to teach reading. *The American Spelling Book* was based on the idea that "reading" (defined as oral rather than silent) was a matter of pronouncing words, spelled aloud syllable by syllable, and once pronounced correctly, would result in understanding. While the method worked, the intensive phonic drills and workbooks wearied the young reader and reading came to be associated with something unpleasant.

The look-and-say method

Sight reading was promoted after Noah Webster's Speller was published as a "better" alternative because competitors felt that Webster's approach was unnecessarily complex. Students using the sight-reading method memorize the appearance of words and associate their meaning. The reason sight reading continues to be an option for reading instruction is that it works—at first. Young children are able to memorize words quickly. However, once in 3rd or 4th grade, the 2,000 to 3,000 words previously memorized are insufficient for reading at an advanced level and the child has no way of sounding out new words. The wonderful, rich treasures of literature are closed to these children unless they can learn to decode the words.

In 1955, Rudolf Flesch came out with *Why Johnny Can't Read*, an indictment of the sight-reading method used by most schools at the time. He called for a return to the phonetic method of teaching reading. Many school districts, beginning in the early 1970s, went to a phonics approach. Others used a blended approach of both sight words and phonics. Yet, even so and with millions of dollars poured into reading research, illiteracy, according to the National Assessment of Adult Literacy, continues to rise each year.

What is missing in our reading programs? The context! While children may be able to decode words, what they are offered for reading improvement are low-level books that lack interest and expressive language—an insult to the child's intelligence.

Charlotte Mason and reading

British educational reformer Charlotte Mason addressed beginning reading in her book *Home Education* (1886). Miss Mason advocated the use of sounds and meaning in conjunction with good literature:

> *At this stage, his reading lessons must advance so slowly that he may just as well learn his reading exercises, both prose and poetry, as recitation lessons. Little poems suitable to be learned in this way will suggest themselves at once; but perhaps prose is better, on the whole, as offering more of the words in everyday use ... Short fables, and such graceful, simple prose as we have in Mrs. Gatty's Parables from Nature, and, still better, in Mrs. Barbauld's prose poems [Hymns in Prose for Children], are very suitable. Even for their earliest reading lessons, it is unnecessary to put twaddle into the hands of children.* (p. 204)

Miss Mason called for "living" books to sustain the child's need for nourishing ideas. She called a book living that is well-written and well-told by a single author with a passion for his subject. The key to learning she felt was to provide children access to living books:

> *For this reason we owe it to every child to put him [or her] in communication with great minds that he may get at great thoughts ... and the only vital method of education appears to be that children should read worthy books, many worthy books.* A Philosophy of Education, p. 12

Charlotte Mason's timeless methods are seeing a revival in education in the United States.

A literature approach to reading

During the 1880s, reading instruction in the United States began to include primers that became known as literature readers. Margaret Free, a primary school teacher at Forestville School in Chicago (circa 1898) and Harriette Taylor Treadwell, the principal of West Pullman School in Chicago (no dates given), were the first to use folktales with beginning readers. The folktale was an ideal choice because it was part of the American culture and lent itself to repetitive vocabulary—an early reading strategy still in use today. The first book, *The Primer*, was a graded text for young readers published in Evanston, Illinois, in 1910.

The Primer, First Reader and *Second Reader* were phonics-based literature readers which used quality literature rather than "twaddle," as Charlotte Mason termed dumbed-down texts. Free and Treadwell maintained that reading instruction should be a joyous activity. To achieve that the authors advocated phonics (with some sight words) for early reading, *with one important addition*: their readings start with and continually work from good literature. The phonics instruction would grow from the child's own curiosity and interaction with word-rich literature.

After repeated requests for a guidebook to using the first three readers, the authors created the *Reading-Literature Teacher's Guide*, originally published as *Primary Reading and Literature, A Manual for Teachers to Accompany the Reading-Literature Series*.

The Reading-Literature reader *series* eventually included nine readers and was so successful that numerous editions were produced. Some states, such as California, published their own editions.

Why bring the Reading-Literature Series back into print now?

The Reading-Literature Series should be brought back into print because we still need to give children something wonderful to read, something that develops a love of good literature right from the start. Nearly all reading programs available today focus on either sight-word reading or phonics instruction and they fail to consider the child's interest in and requirement for something worth reading.

Getting the most out of the *Reading-Literature Teacher's Guide*

The *Reading-Literature Teacher's Guide* makes it clear from the first pages that it is not a rigid program, but rather a guide for parents and teachers to develop their own program. Lest that sound overwhelming, Free and Treadwell present very concrete suggestions and steps to follow, including a lesson-by-lesson plan for the beginning reading.

The process consists of the following distinct steps:

- The telling of the story so that each child has the thread of interest.

- The reproduction of the story by the pupils dramatizing it, or one or more telling it.

- The presentation of the sentence, as it appears in the *Primer* story.

- Teaching the individual words of these sentences, from the sentence, as sight words.

- A phonic drill to be given daily after the reading of the first *Primer* story.

As you learn to use the guide and the three readers that accompany it, you will begin to see, as we have, that Free and Treadwell had it right:

*After years of careful work we present these [readers]
so as to utilize the child's love for stories and make an
easy road to reading. Avoiding the long struggle through
forced interest, and the devious byways of artificial
methods, we start the child at once into the realm of good,
appropriate literature.* Preface, *The Primer*

SHEILA CARROLL
MOUNT PLEASANT, MICHIGAN

ORIGINAL INTRODUCTION

The "Reading-Literature Readers," by Free and Treadwell, were not designed to be what is commonly known as "method readers." There were already too many so-called method readers. Most of them have been arranged without reference to child-interest and solely to the end that certain methods might be developed and used.

The "Free and Treadwell Readers" aim first, last, and all of the time to secure and hold the child's interest. They were compiled in the schoolroom from child literature that has held the interest of children through generations that are gone and that will be read with equal interest by millions in the years to come.

In the beginning the publishers had prepared a brief teachers' manual to accompany *The Primer*. Beyond that it was then thought and is yet believed that any good method may be successfully used with these books.

Since the books have become very extensively used it has been found that, owing to widely different degrees and kinds of preparation, many need, or think they need, more help than was provided in the original manual.

The book aims to show teachers how simple and natural are the essential principles of teaching young children to read; to outline clearly and definitely simple methods in harmony with the most approved ideas of teaching reading, yet leaving the directions so flexible that teachers may be strengthened by their helpful guidance rather than hampered and weakened by an artificial, daily routine; and to enlarge the conception of the significance of the best literature in the early years of the child's life.

The manual aims to be suggestive. It is not desired that any teacher follow it slavishly; rather that relatively inexperienced teachers shall find in it helpful guidance. The efficient, progressive teacher is always larger than any method that another can prescribe. Nor is it the purpose here to outline a new and startling plan. The aim is rather to gather and organize the experience of the best primary teachers of recent years, in what may well be called a "combination method."

The methods suggested have been based upon and made to fit the content of the readers—a plan in direct variance with that usually followed, in which the content of the books is prepared to fit a preconceived, artificial method.

The book is offered to teachers, who use and will use the "Free and Treadwell Readers," in the earnest hope that it may serve to make the day's work more joyous; that, through its organization of material, it may lead to a solution of many difficulties; and, finally, that it may help millions of little learners to find their way more easily and more quickly into the delightful realms of bookland.

The basis of this book was "First-Year Reading," prepared by Anna Morse of the Charleston, Illinois, Normal School. Among those who helped in the enlargement and remaking of the book are Supt. W. R. Siders, Pocatello, Idaho; Miss Mary L. Robinson, Peoria, Illinois; Miss Martha Olson, Evanston, Illinois, and Dr. Harriett Ely Fansler, Columbia University, New York.

THE PUBLISHERS

PRIMARY READING AND LITERATURE

GENERAL PRINCIPLES

Primary reading, as is true of all reading, is for the purpose of promoting thought, and right reading habits are laid by first developing an interest in and love for reading. Reading is not, primarily, word study or word recognition. Even the simplest kind of reading means getting thought and feeling from written or printed characters. Oral reading is a still more complex process, involving, not only getting ideas, but all that goes to make oral expression of the thought and feeling. Children are led by desire and interest to get the thought, and the interest is sustained through their love for stories. The most important factor in teaching a child reading is to develop and foster his desire to read. The only means of ensuring these conditions is to provide reading matter that all children enjoy.

The process herein suggested consists of the following distinct steps: the telling of the story so that each child has the thread of interest; the reproduction of the story by the pupils dramatizing it, or one or more telling it; the presentation of the sentence, as it appears in the *Primer* story; teaching the individual words of these sentences, from the sentence, as sight words; and a phonic drill to be given daily after the reading of the first *Primer* story. The first work on phonics will consist of the drills on consonant values in words known to the child. Later, these consonant elements will be used in blending with phonograms to form words. Ultimately, the drill will be in the phonic analysis of the new words as they appear.

SIGHT WORDS

Every teacher knows that once the child has made a beginning, he will recognize many words at sight, from the context. But, relying upon sight-word drill alone has never resulted in independence in the recognition of new words.

1

Therefore, after the first few lessons in *The Primer*, the drill in phonics should begin and should receive constant, systematic, daily attention until the children are able to sound out most new words for themselves.

PHONICS

It is not the purpose here to set forth a "scientific system" of phonics. It is not believed desirable that children in these early grades have even a "complete system" of phonics. It is the aim to give, in this manual, only such work as experience has shown necessary to train children into independent power over words in their reading vocabulary.

There have been complete and scientific systems used for drill in the past. There are such systems yet in use in some sections of the country. But these systems have proved generally unsatisfactory. Their failure may be very clearly traced to the fact that they are too complex and elaborate.

While it is true that the child needs to know the vowel values only as he may find them in combinations, he *must* know all of the consonant values. These should be taught from words which the child knows at sight. True, some of the consonants have more than one value but if those which occur most frequently in his reading are first taught, he will get the others in much the same way that he gains a knowledge of the vowel values—from letter combinations and from context.

Most of the consonants have only a single value. These are *b, d, f, h, j, k, l, m, n, p, qu, r, t, w, y. Wh* as in wheat, *cr* as in cry, *sk* as in sky, *gr* as in ground, *c* (hard) as in Christian, and *s* (sharp) are other values that the child will need for drill in the use of *The Primer*.

DIACRITICAL MARKS

Diacritical marks are used, in the main, to show vowel values. If the varying sounds of the vowels are to be taught, in the abstract, these marks or some similar aid will be necessary. But it is not necessary that the vowel values should be so

2

taught. Indeed, it is not even desirable. It is much better to teach these values in combination with final consonants and in phonograms. In most cases, the consonant or the combination of letters immediately following the vowel will control the value of that vowel. It is better to ignore the use of these marks until about the fourth grade, when the dictionary is brought into use. Then pupils may gain a working knowledge of them in a very few days.

NON-PHONIC WORDS

It may be suggested that these drills will not give power over non-phonic words; but if the child receives regular and thorough training in the essentials of phonics, he can easily be led to use his knowledge, with increasing power, in mastering all new words. However, there is no good reason why such words as will not readily answer to his knowledge of phonics may not be taught as sight words.

A good way to learn to recognize new non-phonic words is to cover or omit the new word, reading the rest of the sentence, then judge what word will fit the context. This plan is strongly recommended because it trains in reading ideas.

In teaching words at sight, the teacher will devise ways of securing repetition. The aim is to get interesting presentations. One good way is to write the word several times in easy sentences, or alone, with colored crayons, etc. Of course, this is drill, and drill may become a mechanical grind. But drill is necessary, and the teacher must exercise her ingenuity to secure variety, so that the work is done in a snappy way. With an indolent and inefficient teacher, any kind of drill is likely to become monotonous.

Teach new words by relating the work to new steps in the story.

Words that have little individual meaning—as conjunctions, some adjectives, prepositions, etc., should be dropped into the thought by making use of them.

EXPRESSION

There can be no reading without the right sort of expression. Children, before entering school, have learned to express themselves in words almost entirely by imitating those with whom they have been most closely associated. They are likely to imitate even the tone and inflection of those for whom they have the greatest affection. This leads, many times, to faulty use of words, wrong pronunciation and peculiar expression, all of which the teacher must gradually and patiently correct.

Reading is getting and expressing thought and feeling. The effort of the teacher, therefore, must be to lead the child to get thought and feeling, and then good expression will usually come naturally.

The following principles are essential in the teaching of Primary reading, and the Primary teacher should study what here follows until she knows the ideas as well as she knows the multiplication table.

1. The child should learn to read as naturally as he learns to talk and for exactly the same reason—a desire to find out something, or a desire to tell something.

Poor expression is the result of imperfect comprehension of the thought. There must be preparation on the thought before trying to read. The children must be taught to look ahead and catch the thought of the whole combination of words. Until this is possible, the exercise is only one in word-calling—not reading. If the child is free, unrestrained, he can express his ideas and feeling as well as anyone.

2. Assigning to different children parts of stories, dialogues, or poems in an aid in securing right expression. Occasionally the teacher may read one part of a story or dialogue while children take the other parts.

3. Children may be allowed, or asked, to read to the entire school. The reader stands before the school, while all give attention. He must read with expression in order that he may be understood, because the other children have no books open before them. At first, only the best readers should be allowed to read to the school, but the privilege should gradually be extended to every member of the school.

4

4. If any child expresses the notion that the reading may be improved, in whole or in part, allow *him* to read the story or that part of it in question.

5. Dramatization is one of the best means for securing the right expression, even in middle grades. The stories of the "Free and Treadwell Readers" are especially suitable for dramatization by the children themselves. Different pupils may be required to take different parts in playing these stories and these plays, at different times, should include all of the members of the class, the slowest as well as the brightest.

6. Do not tolerate an unnatural tone of an affected manner. Insist on the children's "telling" their stories, not to the blackboard, nor to the books, but to the teacher, to some particular pupil, or to the entire group.

7. It is a mistake to keep a class too long on one lesson. It is better to go back to it after a time than to read that in which the pupil has lost interest.

8. Do not permit sing-song reading, drawling, shouting, or mumbling. *Tone down* high pitched, shrill voices to a natural tone.

9. The voice should receive attention from the first and all proper effort should be made to help the child to control and improve it for expressing thought in his own or the author's words. Drills for enunciation and articulation will be needed in every grade.

10. The teacher may read to the school. Sometimes, the story period is fixed immediately to follow the opening of the school sessions and, because of the children's interest, it becomes a strong, wholesome incentive to punctuality.

HELPFUL MATERIALS

Certain materials for the use of the teacher and the pupils will be found very helpful when properly used. The publishers of the "Reading-Literature Readers" furnish these helps at a nominal price; but the teacher, if she will, can make for herself all of these and others that her experience will suggest. A description of these devices follows:

Perception Cards. This set consists of one hundred sixty cards, each card containing one of the words taught in *The Primer*. The cards may be used in teaching the new words of a story, in word drills and in testing quick recognition of words already taught. In using the cards for quick recognition, the teacher will stand before the class with the cards in her hands. These she will display, one at a time, for quick recognition. At first, this work should be done somewhat slowly, so that all children may have a part in the word recognition, but later, the drill should be rapid. In the beginning, only two or three of the cards will be used, but others will be added to the pack as the vocabulary increases.

These cards are 4 by 6 inches in size and they may be made by any teacher. This diagram shows the plan.

rat

Pupil's Word Cards. These consist of a set of thirteen cards, each containing seventy words. These are the words of *The Primer* and every word is repeated several times. The words are printed between lines so that they may be cut out along the lines, in uniform size. Thus every child may have all of the words of *The Primer* repeated several times. They may be kept in envelopes or in small boxes, and are to be used by pupils in their seats in sentence building.

In the beginning, this sentence building will consist simply of following or copying sentences with *The Primer* open before the pupil. Later, sentences may be built from dictation.

Any teacher who has access to a typewriter [computer and printer] can make these cards.

hen	pig	bread	cat
dog	send	wheat	found
plant	cut	thresh	grind
	make	eat	

Phonic Cards. These are a set of 21 cards, 4x6 inches
in size, for the use of the teacher in drilling on the consonant
elements. They are printed on both sides. On one side is the
words containing the consonant, slightly separated from the
phonogram. Just below is the consonant alone. On the reverse
side of the card, the consonant is printed in both capital and
lower case forms. The appearances of one of these cards is here
shown.

The child knows the word "red" at sight. The teacher
may first write or print the word on the blackboard, with the
consonant slightly separated from the rest of the word. If the
child does not, at first, readily recognize the word, a line may
be made to connect its parts. When it is recognized, the line
should be removed an the children led to say the parts of the
word as they appear upon the blackboard. After a few such drills
from the blackboard, with the first few words, the cards alone
will suffice. The subsequent drill from the cards will be on the
consonants alone, as they appear on the reverse side. In this
drill, if the child does not readily recognize the consonant, the
teacher may turn the card over and require him to work out the
consonant from the word, as in the beginning. Drill on consonant
elements should be daily and continuous until children are
thoroughly familiar with them.

WORKING PLANS

The stories used in these readers are worth lingering over and rereading, and the pupils should not be hurried through the books. The repetition, if at all lively and wide awake on the part of the teacher, is attractive to the child.

The stories are suitable as a real basis for many kinds of lessons, and this manual directs attention to the following:

Language

1. Hearing and telling the stories.

2. Playing or dramatizing the situations when possible.

3. Memorizing stories and poems wholly or in part.

Reading

1. Blackboard sentences based on the stories.

2. Blackboard sentences based on dramatization.

3. The use of the book itself.

4. The use of printed words and sentences chosen from the vocabulary in the book.

5. The use of phonics all the time.

Drawing

1. Illustrative—original drawings representing incidents.

2. Formal—tracing pictures, coloring outlines prepared by the teacher.

Clay and Sand Work

1. Modeling simple figures mentioned in the stories.

2. Staging the actors on the sand-table.

Nature Lessons

About animals and plants mentioned.

Room Decoration

Use of pictures and cuttings relating to the literature.

PURPOSES

The varied lessons to which this manual directs attention have a twofold purpose:

First, to add to the child's general culture.

Second, to enrich the process of learning to read. Since reading involves more that is new and difficult to a child than anything else in the first year of school, most of this part of the manual is devoted to that subject.

GENERAL SUGGESTIONS FOR BEGINNING

I. **Telling the Story.** Teacher should know the original story and adapt it, keeping the *Primer* story in mind as a guide when she prepares her story.

II. **Conversation about the Story.** Free expression on the part of pupils and teacher gives an insight into the understanding of the story, a chance to correct mistaken notions, and helps pupils to gain information which they need to make a unified whole of the story.

III. **Dramatization of the Story.** This should be begun early in the development of the new story. It aids the pupils in getting the setting of the story, vitalizes the thought, gives opportunity for self-activity and self-expression. The child lives the thought through its dramatization, and later, when he reads it his expression will likely be better because of this experience.

Too much emphasis cannot be placed upon the manner of dramatization. The inexperienced teacher often errs in giving too much direction for it. Bear in mind these facts; tell your story clearly, picture vividly the images you wish the pupils to get, question in such sequence as to secure continuity of thought in the reproduction, and, when you feel that the children have the story well in mind, parts in proper relation, say, "Would you like to make up a game about the Little Red Hen, and see if we can play it?"

Assign the various parts and allow pupils freedom in arranging the stage. If the teacher remembers only to direct and allow the pupils to do the acting, her dramatization will be a joy and a source of excellent results by way of laying a foundation for individual expression.

IV. **Reference to Sentence.** The teacher should write on the blackboard the sentence as given in the book. She should then read it, sliding the pointer under it as she reads. A number of children should then each read it, again sliding the pointer under the sentence. This will tend to the establishment of smooth reading.

v. Locating of Word in the Sentence. Find the word *hen*, or find the sentence, *The little red hen found a seed.* The pupil slides the pointer under the sentence, saying it as a whole, not as unrelated words. Then the teacher says, "Which word is hen?" Until his knowledge of phonics can guide him, the pupil may read silently to find the word.

vi. Use of Print and Script. Unless she can letter well, the teacher should not use the print forms on the board; it is simply an added difficulty to the pupils. If the teacher uses the script on the board pupils can take perception cards to the blackboard and match with script there.

vii. Rearrangement of Words into unfamiliar Sentences. These sentences should be written upon the board. They should not be contradictory to the facts of the story in the book.

viii. Silent Reading. The best materials for this are sentences giving directions to be read silently and acted out by the pupils, as in the *Little Red Hen*—

> *You may be the hen, Mary.*
>
> *You may be the cat, Fred.*
>
> *John may be the dog.*

Or in *The Boy and the Goat*—

> *Play you are the boy, Jack.*
>
> *You may be the goat, Albert.*
>
> *You may be the squirrel, Grace.*

ix. Oral Reading. Pupils should not be asked to express themselves orally until they have looked the sentence through and are sure of the thought. Then, looking from the book, they should tell the teacher or the classmates what they have prepared.

x. Pupils tell the Story. After the pupils have read the story for themselves, two, three, four, even more, if the interest be sustained, should be allowed to tell it to the class, to a visitor, or to another class in the building.

XI. Enunciation. First of all the teacher should set a good example in clear enunciation. Hold pupils responsible for making the classmates understand what is said. The teacher should keep at a distance from the one who is reading.

Making a list of words which pupils do not enunciate properly and having a drill separate from the reading lesson time but referring to this list when a mistake is made, is invaluable. Working with individuals who seem to be slow to hear differences in sounds, finding out the cause of the difficulty, may be time well spent.

XII. Phonics. Phonic drills should always be separate from the reading period, but phonics should be used as soon as pupils have the power to get new words of the reading lesson. A drill on the new words should always be given previous to the reading. An exhaustive list of words in a family, or set of words, containing the same phonogram, is unnecessary. Four or five words are sufficient.

Words that are outside the child's vocabulary should not occur in these lists. Meaningless combinations which are neither words nor phonograms should not be used merely for the sake of phonic gymnastics.

XIII. Time and Number of Reading Lessons. Children should have two or three short reading lessons daily and two or three drills in phonics of two to five minutes each. These periods should be full of vivacity and enthusiasm. Short lessons are better than long ones, for little children are likely to become fatigued if kept long at one task. The time devoted to reading the lesson as well as to phonic drills may be extended as children grow in power of sustained attention.

XIV. Devices. 1. Use the Perception cards for the purpose of drilling upon the words.

2. Use as sentence builders, cards containing the words written or printed on them. Let these be put together so as to form the easy sentences of the chart or board lessons.

3. Assign expression work to occupy the pupils at their seats. This must be some profitable employment. Playing with sticks, marking with a pencil, or doing anything else with no definite aim in view, should not be permitted. The work should be copying, illustrating by drawing, or painting, card work, paper folding, making objects described in the reading lessons, etc.

4. If desired, a chart for the reading work can be made from card stock or poster board. Use a thick, black marker, making letters that can be seen across the room. Teachers are advised to depend upon the board and methods suggested heretofore rather than upon the chart.

5. Fasten to the top of the blackboard a common window shade with a spring roller. This is to be used to cover lessons written on the board for sight reading.

6. Use colored chalk on the blackboard to emphasize certain words or ideas.

7. Print the sentences on long strips of card stock (which may be glued onto stiff cardboard, if you wish).

Specific Suggestions and Directions

The more detailed suggestions regarding method in beginning reading are arranged in four sections:

Use of Book from the First

Section I *(PAGE 15)* aims to give specific directions for those teachers who desire to place the book in the hands of the pupils within the first week. This was the intention of the authors of *The Primer*. So far as is known the plan has proved satisfactory wherever tried. The delight the little folk feel when they realize they can read a story from the book is beyond description.

An Alternate Plan

Section II *(PAGE 37)* is simply an alternate plan for the guidance of those teachers who prefer to postpone having the children read from the book for about three weeks. There is no serious objection to this plan. For some teachers, with certain types of children, it may be the better plan. It is, however, likely to involve a large amount of unnecessary work, that is distinctly less interesting than that involved in the plan outlined in Section I.

Supplementary Reading

Section III *(PAGE 45)* presents suggestions regarding the selection and use of supplementary reading.

The Course in Phonics

Section IV *(PAGE 49)* is designed to give all the help any teacher needs for systematic and thorough teaching of all the essentials of phonics.

SECTION I

PUPILS USE *THE PRIMER* FROM THE FIRST

THE LITTLE RED HEN

The teacher tells the children the story, as a whole. She uses good English, vivid description, simple natural dialogue, but does not confine herself to the text of *The Primer*. She lets the children talk about the story, draw pictures, and dramatize the incidents told. This precedes the reading lesson which comes at a later time during the day.

First Reading Lesson

The teacher recalls the story by means of a question or two, and writes, as plain as print, *The Little Red Hen*, upon the board. She tells the children the whole group of words, not trying to separate it in their minds into words nor to drill upon it at all—merely to let the children know she has written the name of the story. Later, when she wishes to use these words in her conversation, she takes care to point to the whole group on the blackboard as she speaks it. She opens a primer before the pupils, teaches them how to hold a book and turn the leaves. Then, pointing to the group of words on the board, she says, "I'll show you a picture of *the little red hen*," and turns to page 1. She then gives a book to each pupil. Each is to keep his book closed until told otherwise. When all are ready, the teacher points again to the board, and says, "Find a picture of *the little red hen* on the inside of your book," writing instead of speaking the name, *The Little Red Hen*. "Find the very first picture of this," pointing again to the name. "Show me her name on the page."

"What does it say?" The name of the story may be written three or four times, in different colors.

15

This may be followed by writing on the board the name of the child the teacher wishes to gather and put away the books. Then she writes the word, *Rise*, if she wishes the pupils to go to their seats; at first speaking the word each time she refers to the board, later pointing to the word instead of speaking it.

Second Lesson

The teacher steps to the board and writes, *The Little Red Hen*. "This is the story I'm thinking about," pointing instead of speaking the name. The children will probably read the name of the story. If they do not, the teacher may show the tiniest glimpse of the picture on page 1 in *The Primer*. The teacher commends those who know the story she had in mind and then erases the words. "Now I'm thinking about this story," she says, as if she meant another one, and writes the same title on the board. She remembers that often repeated experiences are necessary to impress images of words upon the minds of little children learning to read.

Some children can tell at once. But for others, she writes again in another place on the board, *The Little Red Hen*, and says, "What does this make you think of?" She gives the slower ones a chance to tell. The teacher then holds up a strip of paper on which she has written, *The little red hen found a seed*. "This tells what she found," she says, and several children read it. The teacher then writes the same sentence on the board. "Can you read *this*?" she asks. Some child probably can do so, but not everyone in the class. "See what this says"—and she writes the same sentence under the first. She writes this same thing perhaps half a dozen times on the board, in such a way that like words come one under another—and until the class see the likenesses.

Then, when all are expecting the same sentence to appear once more, she writes a different one, *It was a wheat seed*, and looking expectantly toward the class asks, "Who can read this?" Some will at once respond, "The little red hen found a seed!" The teacher leads them to see the joke she played on them when they were not expecting it. "I wrote something different this time. See how it begins—not at all like *The Little*"— pointing to these words as she speaks them. "I said, '*It was a wheat seed*.' You see the last part is just the same. That is the word *seed*. Here it is

16

again where we said, 'The little red hen found a *seed.*' Can you see it anywhere else on the board?"

Then she closes the lesson by asking various children to erase certain sentences from the board, pupils at seats clapping if the child at the board touches and erases the correct sentence.

Third Lesson, Page 2

Before class time the teacher has written on the board,

The	little	red	hen	found	a	seed.
The	little	red	hen	found	a	seed.
The	little	red	hen	found	a	seed.
It	was	a	wheat		seed.	
It	was	a	wheat		seed.	
seed	seed	seed	little	little		
found	found	found a seed				

The arrangement of these sentences and of the words for drill should be varied.

"Find some words that look alike to you," she directs some child. She shows what she means by a *word*, by pointing not to the center nor to the beginning of the group of letters, but by moving the pointer under the whole word, or by putting her two hands around the word.

After the children have pointed to various groups of similar words (not *naming* them, for they are not expected to recognize isolated words yet) the teacher says, "If I should tell you one word, you could know whenever I was writing about that thing. Here is *seed*. Where else was I thinking seed? Here is all I said that time," pointing to the sentence written first, and reading aloud, "The little red hen found a seed." "Did you hear that word *seed* as I spoke? It was the last one I said—and the last one I wrote. Can you find which part of the sentence says *red? little?*" Carry this device as far as seems advisable.

Do not teach the words *the* and *a* as isolated words. Directions like this should be given: Find *a* seed, or find *The little red hen.* Which word is *red?* Which is *hen?* Which is *little?*

17

It is unnecessary to separate *a, the*, and *an* from the names, for these words recur so often they practically teach themselves, if just slipped in by the teacher when necessary, as *a seed, the little red hen*. There is much danger of too great importance and stress being placed upon these words, thereby spoiling the expression in oral reading.

This is not meant for a drill, and the teacher must not expect pupils to remember the words. It is merely a voyage of discovery in which the children who have so far thought in sentences now discover that a sentence can be separated into words.

The class is dismissed by allowing the pupils to take turns in reading a sentence as the teacher erases it from the board, thus saving their time and hers.

Fourth Lesson, Page 2

Before class time the teacher has printed on strips of card stock the two sentences used in writing the day before, and also the separate word *seed*, and the title, *The Little Red Hen*. This last she holds up and asks the children to find in the book where it says, *The Little Red Hen*, pointing to her printed words as she speaks. "Point to the next place where it says,—" and she does not speak the phrase as she holds up the paper. "I see a little *seed* (holding up word) in the picture. This is the name. You may touch the picture. Find the word *seed* under your picture. It looks like this word, only smaller ... Find the word *seed* in another place." During this time the teacher moves about among the children, showing them several words like hers.

Holding up her first printed slip she says, "Find in your books a sentence that looks like this. It says, '*The little red hen found a seed.*' Find another line just like it ... What does that say?" asks the teacher of several children. Then she treats the other lines on the page in a similar way. As a summary of the lesson, she stands behind the class, where she can see as many individuals as possible, and reads a sentence at a time, seeing that they show where their books say what she speaks.

Fifth Lesson, Page 3

"Play you are the little red hen, Anne," says the teacher, pointing, as she speaks them, to the underlined words which she has written on the board. A few grains of wheat have been scattered about on the floor before the class, and Anne hunts about and finds one, saying, "Who will plant the seed?" "What did she find, Isabel?" asks the teacher. "I'll write it here on the board." *The little red hen found a seed*— she writes. "Read this sentence, Miriam—Russel—Ruth."

"What kind of seed was it, Little Red Hen?" she asks, turning to Anne.

"It was a wheat seed," the child answers. "I'll write that on the board," says the teacher, as she begins.

"Read this sentence, James—Russel—Helen." "Read both these sentences, Edwin."

"What did the little red hen say, Katherine?" asks the teacher, pointing to the sentences as she speaks it. Children answer, and teacher writes, *The little red hen said, "Who will plant the seed?"* Different children read and reread the various sentences on the board, and when the class turns to go to their seats, each child points to some word or sentence or phrase on the board as he goes by—the teacher giving a hint as she gives her directions, by saying, "I don't know what word you'll choose to touch and tell. Perhaps you'll point to *seed* (doing so herself as she speaks), or perhaps you'll choose *plant* (pointing to the word), or it may be you'll point to *The little red hen*—you see I don't know. You are to decide." Then children in turn march past the board and back to their seats, touching and pronouncing "their words" as they go.

Sixth Lesson, Page 3

The teacher has prepared, by use of the computer, or carefully hand lettered, the printed sentences used on page 3. She holds up the first and asks some child to read it. Possibly he cannot, or attempts and guesses wrong. The teacher reads it correctly, saying, perhaps, "Now, next time you'll know. See this beginning part—*The—little—red—hen*. And here is this last word *seed*. Remember. What does this say?" Then, laying down the printed slip with the others—and seeming to pick up another she asks, "Read what this says, Alice," showing the same sentence. This device is often used, until pupils recognize likenesses and can tell every time when the teacher makes this kind of test. After using all the sentences on the page in this way, with large printed slips, the teacher asks the pupils to open their books at page 3 and read the same sentences from the book. While one child reads, the others show where it says the same thing in their books. The notion that there is value in having one child *tell* the others a sentence whose content is already perfectly familiar—while they sit with closed books and assume an interest they do not feel—is an exploded idea. It is only the form on page 3 that is new, and this form must appeal to the eye, not the ear; therefore the children ought to be using their eyes while they *are* listening to one child read.

Seventh Lesson, Preparing for Page 4

The teacher stands at the board before the class and says—writing italicized words neatly but quickly as she speaks them—"Today we shall *plant* some wheat seeds as the little hen did—only ours must be in these little boxes" (one for each child). (See suggestions for hand work on page 38.) "Here is the *seed. Who will plant the seed?* Play you are the *cat*, Anne. Play you are the *pig*, Kate. Play you are the *dog*, Vera. This is what each one said when the hen asked, *'Who will plant the seed?'* ... *'Not I,' 'Not I,' 'Not I.'*"

"Play you are *The Little Red Hen*, Frances. Ask your friends, *'Who will plant the seed?'*" Children answer as teacher points, or point and answer—"*Not I.*" *The little red hen said, "I will,"* writes the teacher as Frances answers her friends. "You may *plant the seed* in your box, Frances." Frances plants several seeds. Then other children play they are the different animals mentioned and as the lesson proceeds, different ones point to their names or to their conversation on the board as this little incident in the story is acted and re-acted, and various "little red hens" plant the seeds in their boxes. If time is short, the teacher may say the parts for the pig, the cat, and the dog, writing or pointing as she speaks, while all who are left may play they are a whole flock of "little red hens" and answer all at once as they plant the wheat.

Eighth Lesson, Page 4

Let the memory of the story help the children enjoy this
page. It will be partly guessing and partly reading. The teacher
must lead the pupils to guess correctly at this stage of reading.
You may rest assured that the work in phonics, if well taught,
will do away with any need for guessing a little later in the
term.

Each child opens his book to the page. "Let us tell the story
from the picture first. Who talked first? ... What did she say?
... "I'll show you where the reading on the page tells that very
thing!" Then she turns her book to show the pupils the very
thing they have told from the picture.

"Here is the fellow who spoke next," she says, pointing to the
picture of the pig. "What did he say?" She may need to reword
the child's answer to fit the wording of the next sentence—"Yes,
the pig said, 'Not I.' ... Here is where the book tells about it,"
and she points to the sentence ... "Who spoke next? Show me her
picture. What did she say? Here it tells that very thing. Let's all
say it. Show me where it is in your book. Now read what the dog
said ... I'll read the last line on the page."

Then the teacher goes about behind the different members
of the class and asks them to show her where it says, "Not I, Not
I, Not I," on the page. She directs them to find the same thing
on page 5, saying, "That tells the next part of the story when the
little red hen asked them to do some other work for her."

Ninth Lesson, Review

Children use books, "reading" page 1, looking at the first line
on page 2, and then telling it. The teacher may stop here and
ask pupils to point out the words *seed*, *little*, and *wheat* using
perception cards to show the words to all while she does so.

By questioning, lead the pupils to look through each
sentence on the page and then read it aloud. Then without
questions, let some pupil read the whole page, telling him at
once the sentences he does not know. Of course, just here, pupils
can sometimes "read the story" quite as well without the book,
but that does not matter. The point is, can he show where, on
the page, the familiar thought stands? Treat the next two pages

in the same way, and see to it that each child has a chance to read aloud in the recitation many times, occasionally in concert—but usually alone.

Tenth Lesson, Page 5

Caution—Do not hurry to drill on separate words. Do not try to teach these lessons as you yourself were taught to read, unless you are *sure* it was the best way.

The teacher begins, "Look at the picture. This wheat is taller than that we planted. What does the hen want the pig to do now?" Books are laid aside and attention given to blackboard lesson at this point.

"I'll tell you what she said"—(writing) *The little red hen*— (stops to ask—"Who is this?") *said, "Who will cut the wheat?"* "This is who spoke next."

The pig ... (Who is this?)

The cat ...

The dog ...

"Tell me the names of these three animals. Point to *The pig. The cat. The dog* ... Shut your eyes while I write something." ... The teacher writes these groups of words in different places on the board. Then the children open their eyes and she directs— "Find another place where I wrote *The cat*. Where does it say *The pig?*"—pointing to words as she speaks, so that pupils have something by which to test their search. Their own mental images of the words may be too confused and indistinct. The teacher will save time if she finds excuses for telling these words over and over again in an interesting way, and seeing that the children strengthen and deepen the correct image of word, phrase, or sentence. If she expects to tell once, and then test memory on the strength of that one impression, she will meet disappointments, and will lose the confidence of her pupils, who feel she has led them into deep water and left them helpless.

To Finish the First Story

For the following pages of the story let the pictures help tell the new thought—"*Who will thresh the wheat?*" "*Who will grind the wheat?*" etc.—and let a varied repetition in script and print gradually make the child sure of these and the other often repeated sentences from page 1 to page 10.

If a child does not recognize familiar words in new positions on new pages, turn to review pages which he knows thoroughly and show him where it says the very same thing. *Tell* him only so much as is really necessary. Let him stretch his effort to the utmost, but be sure he succeeds in the end.

When the children can read a story *well*, they may be allowed to take their books home to read to Mother and Father or to other children. This will give much practice in oral reading with a genuine motive.

The same order of work as outlined with the first story may be followed, in a general way, with each of the *Primer* stories. After pupils have a sufficient sight vocabulary, the teacher should not tell the story. Let the children have the pleasure of getting its thought by their own effort. The general order, however, should be as follows:

1. Teacher tells the story.

2. Reproduction by the children.

3. Dramatization.

4. Reading sentences from the board and finally, the story.

5. Drill with perception cards on the *Primer* stories, as they are taught: This drill should be thorough, that it will not be required after *The Primer* is completed. Meantime, the child's growing knowledge of phonics should enable him to master most new words as they appear in the lessons.

6. Drill with phonic cards. This work should begin with the second story and these cards should be used for drill until pupils are thoroughly familiar with all consonant elements.

THE GINGERBREAD BOY

As with the first story, the teacher tells the children the story, as a whole, but not confining herself to the text of *The Primer*. She lets the children talk about the story, draw pictures, and dramatize the incidents told. This precedes the reading lesson which comes at a later time during the day.

Preparation, Page 15

Let the first presentation here be from the blackboard. Italicized words are written on board—others spoken.

"I'll tell you more about *The Gingerbread Boy*. The gingerbread boy met *a cat.*

He told the cat who he was. He said—

'I am a gingerbread boy. I am. I am. I am.'

"Play you are the gingerbread boy. Tell us who you are" (pointing to sentence while child repeats).

"What did you do?" Writes as child says—

"I ran away. I ran away from the little old woman. I ran away from the little old man. I ran away. I ran away. I ran away."

"This is what he told the cat"—(teacher reads as she writes—)

"I can run away from you. I can, I can, I can.

"Find where it says, *I can. I can run away from you.*" Teacher reads and writes—

"And he ran, and he ran, and he ran."

She then goes back over the lesson on the board, hinting at how easy it will seem, now that they know what is there. She questions just enough to keep the children reading intelligently—not holding them for a knowledge of many separate words, but knowing that frequent repetition, *if interesting,* will do the work, and children will be reading before they know it.

Further Preparation, Pages 15 and 16

The teacher prints the sentences in large letters on strips of paper five inches wide and a yard or more long [you can tape 11" or 14" pieces of paper together to form the strip], uses the "Perception Cards" or the blackboard. She questions carefully, and shows a sentence suggested by the question for all the class to see. After it is ready by several it is put aside, to be picked up in a moment, and again shown to the class, while the image is fresh in their minds. Again and again the same sentence is shown—until the children know it promptly at sight.

Then the book is opened and the children have the fun of finding themselves able to "read the story."

Similar preparation should be given for pages 17-24. No page in the book should be attempted until there has been:

1. Careful introduction to the thought, usually with blackboard, because here class and teacher come nearer to each other.

2. Enough word-drill so that the recognition of sentences in the book is a pleasurable experience.

3. Enough imagination stimulated through the pictures, the dramatization, the dialogue, to keep the story alive.

While the children are reading the second story, teach consonant elements as follows:

   r in r ed   **h** in h en   **p** in p ig

The child knows these words at sight. When red is placed on the board as r ed, he may not recognize it; but if a line be made to connect the parts, he will, in most cases, readily say the word. This connecting line will not be needed after a very few words are studied in this way.

The Old Woman and the Pig

This story should be told to the children and retold by them, at the story hour or language period, before the reading begins, because there are several words and phrases not in the speaking vocabulary of the ordinary child. Drawing pictures and playing parts of the story add interest on the part of the children, and give the teacher greater opportunity to correct wrong images the child may have formed through hearing the spoken words.

When this has been done, the preparation needed on the form side is much lessened. The preliminary blackboard work may not be shortened to merely a word-drill—as in the lessons previously outlined. A list of words already learned should be kept on the board and children should be drilled on this list as well as with the perception cards.

Devices for conducting this word-drill:

The teacher tells the children to find the first word. She has some child find the word in another place. Tell the children to find the second word.

Then ask another child to tell all the words he knows from the board. The drill may be thus extended, or the teacher may give occasional concert drills as follows:

1. She touches a word with the pointer, and waits until all see. Children keep silent but alert. As soon as she removes the pointer, *all* speak with great *promptness*. Concert drills thus conducted give slower members of the class a fair chance, and promote self-control in the quicker members who want to tell everything.

2. She points to a word with her eraser. All look and keep silent. When the eraser moves over the word, all speak.

When the children are ready to read page 26, the teacher has at hand the list of words printed in large type two inches high and just before the children read each sentence she shows for a second one or two of the key words of that sentence—thus giving a hint of what it is to tell them.

At the end of the lesson the teacher should give short, quick drills on these words, and perhaps lend them to some child to take home and tell his mother.

"Be sure to tell her it is not a spelling lesson!" she warns him—for most well-meaning mothers are strong on teaching spelling, before it is wanted or needed.

After a page has been worked out sentence by sentence, it should not be dropped and forgotten. It should be re-read as a whole by several children, and gone back to in subsequent lessons to be read "just for fun," and "to make it sound like a story."

But in every lesson there should be some *new work*; either words and thoughts not given before, or so differently arranged that they seem new to the children. It is only by pushing *forward* that the teaching of reading is accomplished.

As indicated, drill in the Phonic Series should begin with the third story and should develop as indicated in various suggestions that follow.

The phonic drills beginning with the third story will be on *n* in *not*, *d* in *day*, *y* in *you* and c in *cat*. Give frequent drills, also on the first four Phonic Series while the pupils are reading this story.

Cautions

1. Do not rearrange sentences so that they are contradictory to the facts in the story, merely for the sake of word drill. For example, such sentences as these should not be given: *The little red hen did not find a seed*, or *The little red hen said, "Not I."*

2. Above all, do not measure your success by the number of words your pupils know, nor judge the work of the first year by the number of books read, but by the ease with which the pupils attack new material.

The Boy and the Goat

Some teachers prefer not to tell this story before reading it. The pictures, the words already fairly familiar, and the rapidly growing desire and ability on the part of the pupils to find out new words and sentences for themselves by means of phonics, will more and more do away with the need for blackboard preparation for each page, and for oral introductions. The teacher must come less and less between the child and the book, if reading is taught effectively.

The phonic work to be carried on concurrently with the reading of this story is on *m* in *man*, *s* in *so*, *b* in *but*, and *th* in *then*. At the same time take the next four of the Phonic Series. Remember that in extending the work with these Series, there should be constant review of Series already taught.

This story of the boy and the goat is an excellent one to play. The dialogue is natural and the action rather funny. Written suggestions, taking words or sentences from the story, may be used to start the play, but if used throughout the lesson are too likely to hamper freedom of action and original expression.

The Pancake

By this time the children should have considerable power to recognize words. It should not be necessary to tell this story as a whole before reading begins, for then the incentive for discovering thought for themselves is taken away from the pupils.

Through use of the pictures, hint just enough to lead the children into each page. They will partly guess at the reading there, but they must be made to be sure when they are right by verifying or disproving their guesses by sounding the words.

Example: At beginning of the lesson the teacher may say:

"This tells about an old woman and all her children. How many do you suppose she had?" Children probably count and answer "seven." Read the first sentence and see what the book says. Children then read, first silently, then orally. "What word makes you sure how many there were?" Children point to the word seven.

"What has she on the board?" asks the teacher, referring again to the picture. Guesses are made and then the children are told to find out what the second sentence really tells. The word is the name of the story.

Then after two sentences have been studied through, another child is called upon to read both. Then a third is approached, and so the story grows. After the first three pages have been thus developed sentence by sentence, the rest of the story will need less questioning, for continued repetition will add to the number of words known at sight, and the cumulative thought will make it much easier to infer what is coming next. So questions may tell less, and only direct—for example: "See what happened next," or "what did he say after that?"

This is a well-arranged story, as are many of those in the book, for getting good groupings of words. For example, *"for the boy, into the word, over the brook,"* etc., should be glanced at as a single word and not spoken one at a time. With careless teaching, one rather bad habit may be formed. That is, children may learn to drop their voices after the word *said* when it introduces someone's conversation. This, however, may easily be guarded against if the pupils are trained to read thoughts as wholes.

This grouping of words or "phrasing" is one of the very best aids in securing expression and it should have constant attention.

In fact nothing less than this is reading. The teacher who accepts less is not teaching reading.

The phonic drills with this story are *f* in *fox, t* in *to, g* in *get* and *k* in *kill.* Add to this, drills in Phonic Series nine to twelve, inclusive, with reviews of Series already taught.

CHICKEN LITTLE

This story needs little development beyond the second page, except a naming by the teacher of the characters as they appear

29

in the pictures. The names given in nursery rhymes vary, and a class of children may have quite a variety to suggest if left to guess. Teachers must remember that one "right-telling" is not enough to make up for three or four "wrong-tellings" on the part of classmates.

In using the review stories, for example, page 76 (which is the summary of *Chicken Little*), after a study lesson with the teacher, in which questions, word drills, and phonics help the children to find out what the page says, the teacher may profitably plan a seat lesson in silent reading something as follows:

Each child is supplied with a piece of drawing paper and a soft pencil.

The teacher goes about from seat to seat, encouraging and teaching the individuals, whose different conceptions of the story will be amazing and interesting.

Each child is directed to read a little, until something reminds him of a good picture to draw. Then he is to stop and make the picture—read again, draw another and so on. The pictures will tell whether pupils have really read, and how they interpreted their reading.

This may be varied by having pupils cut the pictures from paper, free hand, instead of drawing them. This is desirable in such a story as "The Three Billy Goats Gruff," where the bridge, the hill, the troll, and the goats are easily distinguishable forms. A child likes to have his cuttings recognized.

The phonic drill with the sixth story, *Chicken Little*, will be *cr* in *cry*, *wh* in *why*, and *qu* in *quench*. Add Phonic Series thirteen to sixteen, inclusive, and review all Series already taught.

THREE BILLY GOATS GRUFF

The phonic drills with the seventh story, *Three Billy Goats Gruff*, will be with *ch* in *chicken*, *sn* in *snout*, and *sk* in *sky*. Add to these a thorough review drill in all the Phonic Series already taught.

LITTLE TUPPENS AND
LITTLE SPIDER'S FIRST WEB

By this time pupils should be accustomed to attempting new words without much help from the teacher. However, it is advisable to teach the new words which appear in these stories before attempting the reading, for when the stumbling blocks are removed the appreciation of the story is greater, the pupils enjoy the story, and hence they read better. In teaching the new words, a pupil should never be told the word if he can possibly get it for himself. Though it takes more time, it pays to let the child use his own powers in this work.

While reading the eighth and ninth stories, the consonant drills will be with *gr* in *gruff*, *th* in *thank*, and *tr* in *trip*. Also complete Phonic Series seventeen to twenty, inclusive. Review all Phonic Series including Series one to twenty.

SILENT READING

Silent reading can only be of value when pupils know the words of a story at sight, or can find them out without audible effort. Silent reading is a thing to be taught with care, and with much persistence. It should begin the first days of school and continue throughout the grades. Whispering, or using lips is not silent reading. After sentences, paragraphs, or pages have been worked through for thought, with the teacher's help, there should be thorough drill in glancing through the material. Drills of various sorts should increase the speed with which this can be done. Single sentences on cards or strips of paper are of value here, since they can be held quiet for a second, then removed from view. Finding the place on a page is another good kind of drill.

SEAT WORK SUGGESTED FOR THE CHILDREN

I. WORK BASED ON HANDWORK

1. Draw pictures that will tell parts of the story. The pupils should do this, not by copying someone else's ideas, but by each one showing how he thinks it might have been. Encourage originality here.

Mediums—Charcoal, crayons, soft pencils, or chalk.

2. Cut or tear from drawing paper or ordinary wrapping paper figures showing parts of stories. Mount on suitable background.

3. Color outline pictures the teacher has copied.

4. After a lesson with the teacher on the needed folds and pastings, let children make small paper boxes for holding a little earth in which wheat seeds may be planted. These germinate very quickly, and after they are a few days old, may be carried home in triumph by the "little red hens" who planted them.

5. Children may make of clay various things suggested by the different stories. For example, in connection with *The Gingerbread Boy* they make make:

> The gingerbread boy. The bowl in which the old woman made him. Her rolling pin. The little old woman.

6. The sand-table is a very helpful medium for fixing the scenes of the stories and promoting freedom and originality of expression.

Little Red Hen Story

The sand-table is converted into a barnyard.

a. Cardboard barn made by the pupils is placed in the barnyard.

b. A fence can be made by folding an oblong paper several times and cutting so as to show posts and horizontal boards.

c. The figures in the story can be modeled in clay or cut out of paper. If made from paper, they should be cut free-hand and suitably colored. Make two of each figure, paste together with a wooden paste-splint or strip of stiff cardboard between, protruding an inch so as to make a stem to be stuck into the sand and hold the figures in an upright position.

Gingerbread Boy

Figures cut from paper, either by pattern or free-hand, of the gingerbread boy, old woman, old man, cat, dog, fox, etc., can be treated like those of the preceding story.

The sooner the pupils get to the free-hand cutting, the sooner will their powers of free expression grow. This work may be very crude in the beginning but it is astonishing how their ability to express grows and the sand-table, giving the practical use for these cuttings, encourages the pupils greatly.

The Old Woman and the Pig

A stile is not within the experience of many of the children. Here is a splendid chance to build either a cardboard stile or a wooden one on the sand- table. The scene where "the old woman got home that night" works out well on the sand-table. Her old house, the stile and the old woman leading the pig down the road make a good scene.

Three Billy Goats Gruff

Make a cardboard bridge and cuttings of the three goats. Water can be represented by placing a glass over blue paper. Sand will make a very good irregular coast-line to the river. The hill may be of sand piled up and covered with sawdust dyed green. The goats might be modeled of clay. The bridge then should be modeled of clay to represent a stone bridge. These suggestions are sufficient to show the possibilities of the sand-table, with which every primary room should be supplied.

II. Work Based on Word-Forms

1. The teacher may duplicate the sentences on a certain page of *The Primer*, using each sentence several times. If she has a mimeograph at hand this is not hard. These pages are given to the children, at first as a reading lesson in class. Then they take them to their seats and cut the sentences so they stand on separate strips. Each child then places all that are alike in one group, like words one under another. Not only does this care in grouping the sentences and words aid the pupils in distinguishing like words but the teacher can easily inspect the work after it is done

2. These same strips may be placed in envelopes and a few days later, when the child has had more drill on those sentences, he is asked as seat work to look them over, put all he knows in one pile and all he does not know in another.

3. He may be directed to lay them in order, to make a story like the one on the board.

4. He may lay them in order, so as to build a small story of his own—or from memory.

5. Pupils may be tested on the ready recognition of the words of a story studied by referring to the list at the back of the book.

Exercises 1 and 3 may be done when the child does not know a single word at sight, if he can recognize words that are alike; 2 and 4 imply a knowledge of at least part of the words and so are to be later treatments of the same material.

These following devices may be used later with lists of words, either the well-printed ones provided by the publisher of *The Primer* on convenient sheets of paper, or lists based on the lesson of the week, printed by the teacher so they can be cut apart.

1. Finding words alike.

2. Separating known words from unknown.

3. Building sentences when model is given.

4. Building original sentences.

Caution

If this work is worth doing at all, it is worth inspection on the part of the teacher after it is done. The teacher should pass up and down the aisles, commenting upon the neatness and exactness of the work, also teasing the pupils as to the thought they have put upon it, by questioning in this manner. What do these sentences say? What are these words?

III. Work Based on Silent Reading

This should be deferred until the latter part of the first year. Use a review story. Let children read until they find a sentence which suggests a good picture, then stop to make a picture, read a little more, make another picture, etc.

Do not ask children to do much writing for seat work.

Suggestions of General Interest

Let the children plant wheat seeds as suggested above.

Ask them to bring ripened stalks of wheat to school. Show what happens when wheat is threshed.

Grind some grain of wheat between two stones. Sift bran and flour. Show several good pictures of the animals mentioned in the stories as you talk about them, especially if you are teaching where children have little opportunity to know animals well.

Use cuttings of these animals, the best views you can get, for a border along the top of your blackboard, adding to the procession as fast as each new friend comes into the stories. This is well suggested by the grouping of animals on the outside of *The Primer*, and the blackboard parade can be made a real help in holding the interest of the children in the slow-growing ability to read about those friends.

Section II

An Alternate Plan

General Outline

Teach the vocabulary of *The Little Red Hen* and *The Gingerbread Boy* (Word List, page 127). Children should have at least two reading lessons daily from the blackboard and one each for word development and drill. These reading lessons from the board should consist of sentences in which all words taught are used as given in the book, but they may be in different arrangement from the sentences in book. Sentences printed with a sign printer, upon long strips of manila cardboard, the perception cards and word cards should be used also. About three weeks should be spent on the board work.

When all the words of *The Little Red Hen* story have been taught and read in sentences in this way, the children may read the story in the book. Continue in this way through *The Primer. The Gingerbread Boy* will usually take about two and one-half weeks. *The Primer* should ordinarily be finished before January. Then as many good supplementary readers should be read as possible, allowing time for the *Reading-Literature First Reader* to be read by the end of the first year.

In the Language period the teacher should take up the subject of wheat, find out what the pupils know, then adding to their knowledge by having illustrative good masterpiece to show in connection with this literature. The teacher should describe the processes through which wheat goes and what it is made into.

The First Reading Lesson

The teacher tells the story of *The Little Red Hen* to the children. She should keep the sentence form in the book but should enlarge and amplify the story between the sentences. This *Primer* version of the story has purposely been made very brief and simple. Allow the pupils to talk about the story and then say: "This all happened because the little red hen found a seed." Then have several children repeat, "The little red hen found a seed." The teacher may then say: "My chalk will say it," and she writes, *The Little Red Hen found a seed.*

The teacher reads it from the blackboard, sliding the pointer under the writing. Then ask other children to say it, always sliding the pointer underneath. Also, the teacher says, "I shall read it again and I want you to find where it says *seed.*" She reads, pausing slightly before *seed.* One child finds the word, places his hands around it, and tells what he found. Then several children do the same. The teacher says, "Would you know it if I wrote it here?" She writes *seed* in various places on the board, children saying it each time. In passing to their seats, each pupil touches some part of the reading lesson and tells what it is.

Second Reading Lesson

The teacher says, "I am glad (then writes while saying)— *The little red hen found a seed*; for if she hadn't (pointing to the words) *found a seed*, we shouldn't have had this delightful story, and another thing, because (writing sentence again) *The little red hen found a seed* we have learned so much about wheat and bread."

"Now will you tell me what this sentence is? And what is this (pointing to the other just like first)? ... Do you see anything in this sentence that looks like part of that sentence? Let's read to ourselves and see what it is. ... If this word is *seed*, show me another *seed.* ... If this is *found*, where is the other *found*? ... Where is *The little red hen*? ... Where else is *The little red hen*?"

The teacher says, "This hen must have had very sharp eyes to find the seed, for (teacher writes and says) '*It was a little seed*,' and though (writes again) '*It was a little seed*,' she knew it was good for something."

The teacher asks, "Who knows where it tells what kind of seed it was?" A pupil takes the pointer, slides it under the sentence and reads, *It was a little seed.* "Where else does it say that?" Another pupil slides the pointer under the other sentence, reading, *It was a little seed.*

Let us find out what it is. Read silently until you come to the word and then tell it."

If the word is *seed*, ask pupils to find *seed* in the sentence, *The little red hen found a seed.*

If no pupil responds to the teacher's request, she might say, "I see *seed* here. Do you see *seed* in that sentence?"

In closing this lesson a game called "Clean House" is great fun and affords another opportunity of re-reading the sentences. A pupil takes an eraser, goes to the board, tells a sentence he chooses to clean off, and then erases it. Another follows in the same way. This is done until the sentences are all cleaned off.

Any device that secures interested attention upon words and sentences and activity on the part of pupils is good.

The Third Lesson

Commence with a short word-drill on seed, hen, found, little, and wheat.

Then write such sentences as these upon the board:

The hen found a seed.

The little hen found a seed.

The hen found a little seed.

The hen found the seed.

The red hen found the wheat seed.

The hen found the little wheat seed.

The little hen found the seed.

After children have read the sentences, the teacher says, "Find every place it says *seed*." A child takes pointer, runs to the board and every time he points to *seed* he must say the word so his classmates hear him. Another pupil finds the word *hen* as often as he can, and so on.

Fourth Lesson

This is planned to give word drill on *it* and *was*, reviewing other words of previous lesson by means of a game.

39

Write one word at a time upon the board, asking pupils to give it, until the eight words are written. One child is then told to stand in a corner with his back to the class, covering both eyes with his hands. Another pupil is given a pointer and told to point to one of these words. When this has been done, the teacher says, "All right, John," and John, who is in the corner, comes back, takes the pointer and says, pointing to a word, "Is it *hen?*" Class responds, "It is not *hen.*" Then he says, "Is it *little?*" If it is, the others reply, "Yes, it is *little,*" and they clap. If John doesn't find the word in three guesses, the others say, "It is *red.*" Then John points to *red* and pronounces it.

If he can't find *red*, another pupil might show him where it is.

Then the pupils are ready to read from the board such sentences as these, rearranged from the story, but not contradictory to the story.

The hen found the seed.

It was the little seed.

It was the little wheat seed.

The hen found the little wheat seed.

Was it the little red hen?

It was the little red hen.

Fifth Lesson

The teacher says, "I wonder how much you can read of this story." She writes,

The little red hen found a seed.

It was a little seed.

Then she produces the two sentences printed upon manila cardboard and says, "Can you take the printed sentence which says, *It was a little seed,* and hold it under the same sentence at the board?

"Who can match this one?" holding up the other card, *The little red hen found a seed.*

"Tell what it says. Show me *seed* here. Show me *seed* on the board. Show me which part says, *The little red hen.* Where is it

40

on the board?

"Show me *found* on this paper; now at the board." Each time a child finds a word or phrase or sentence he should be required to tell it to the class.

Then take the perception cards, *hen, little, red,* etc. Have pupils match each to the printed word in the sentence. Match each to the written word on the board.

This time in the game "Clean House" each child might erase but a word or phrase.

Sixth Lesson

The teacher says, "What did the little red hen say when she found the seed?"

A pupil—"The little red hen said, 'Who will plant the seed?'"

The teacher writes the sentence and then says, "Find *The little red hen.* Find *seed.* Which part says, *Who will plant the seed?* Read to yourselves until you find *plant.* Where is *plant,* John?"

John takes the pointer and points to *plant.*

"Read to yourselves until you find *who.* Show it to me, Mary."

Mary points to *who.*

The teacher says, "Who said (then writes), '*Not I*'?"

A child—"The pig."

Then teacher makes it read, *The pig said, "Not I."* Then a pupil reads the whole sentence.

"Who else said, '*Not I*'?"

A pupil says, "The cat." The teacher writes *The cat said* before "*Not I.*"

Then the teacher says, "Who else wouldn't work?"

Pupil—"The dog."

Teacher—"What did he say?" Pupil—"Not I."

The teacher then writes, *The dog said, "Not I."*

41

The teacher says, "Which sentence says, *The cat said, 'Not I'?*

"Which part says, *'Not I'?*

"Show me some more *'Not I's'.*"

This should be easily recognized by pupils if the teacher has been very careful to write all these similar groups one below another.

Teacher—"Which word is *cat*? Where is *said*? Show me another *said*, and another."

The other sentences should be dealt with in a similar way. In concluding the lesson use the Clean House game.

Seventh Lesson

As part of the phonic lesson a short drill on the words already studied should be given each day, but sometimes it is well to sharpen the children's wits with a short drill just before the reading lesson.

For example, "What did the (teacher writes and speaks) *cat* say?"

Child—"Not I."

The teacher writes that under *cat*. Pointing to the words, the teacher says, "Who else said, *'Not I'?*"

Child—"The dog."

The teacher writes *dog* under *"Not I."*

Teacher—"Who else refused to work?"

Child—"The pig."

Teacher writes *pig* under *dog*.

Then she reviews the whole sentence, *Who will plant the seed?* by saying, "What did the hen say when the pig said, *'Not I'?*"

Now rearrange the sentences like this and write them upon the board:

"Who will plant the seed?" said the little red hen.

"Not I," said the cat.

"Not I," said the pig.

42

"Not I," said the dog.

Have the children find all the places it says *Not I, said, I.* Find *pig, cat, dog, plant*, etc.

Eighth Lesson

The teacher writes, *The little red hen said, "Who will plant the wheat?"*

A child reads the sentence. Then she writes, *The pig said, "Not I."*

Another child reads this, and so on until she has written what is on page four. The last sentence is new, but it almost teaches itself. Then the children play "Match," that is, matching the printed sentences which the teacher has prepared with the written sentences upon the board. Then find the separate words and match the printed words to the written words upon the blackboard and to the separate words in the printed sentences.

By this time the pupils should be familiar with the seven different sentences. A new game can now be played. It is called "Draw." The teacher holds the printed sentences face down in her hand. Each child draws from her hand a sentence and studies it.

The teacher says, "Sentences over!" which means that the pupils turn the cards face down in their laps and fold their hands. She chooses one pupil at a time to stand before the class, hold his long strip so the pupils can read it, too, and he tells them what his sentence says. If there are not enough sentences to go around, the rest of the class "draw" after this first group have read. This game affords another opportunity for review, but unless there be spice and the spirit of play in the work, review so early does not appeal to the pupils.

From now on the number of sentences grows quite rapidly and each pupil will soon have a different sentence.

This same game can be played with the separate words.

These games and devices are good all through the story of "The Gingerbread Boy."

With the Gingerbread story the phonic drills should begin and they should be followed as outlined in previous pages.

Caution

Do not permit pupils to "read until they make a mistake." Emphasis should not be placed upon words alone, but upon the thought of the sentence. Class criticism which runs to mere fault-finding should not be permitted. An atmosphere of helpfulness and sympathy is what is needed. It is generally better for the teacher to make the criticisms. If the pupil reads too poorly to go on, require him to study the work, and get ready for the oral reading. Say to him, "You haven't the thought, better look again." If he gives the thought correctly but not in the words of the book, say to him, "You have the thought, but exactly how does the book give it?"

Section III

Supplementary Reading

All reading material should stand three tests.

1. Will it increase the child's desire to read?

2. Does it make an appropriate demand for good reading habits and good taste?

3. Does it have an intrinsic value in the subject matter which it presents, or in the emotions which it is capable of arousing in children?

Silent Reading

Silent reading should have the first place in the supplementary reading. Someone has said, "Silent reading is the agency which enables the child to look through the words to the thought in the same way that one looks through a clean window glass to the objects beyond."

Silent reading is the only way to teach rapid reading, because a child is not hindered by the agencies he uses when reading aloud. When the child acquires facility in word-recognition he is likely to read aloud too rapidly. It also is an aid in discipline; it helps the teacher to save her voice for a time when it is more necessary to talk; it makes an excellent medium of communication. It is now generally conceded that the more a teacher talks the more she must talk and the less is her power in the schoolroom.

The following examples show how silent reading may be used at a very early stage:

I. This lesson can be given for a class who are to leave the seats and go to the front of the room for a lesson. The teacher writes:

1. *Stand.*

2. *Drum, George.* (George runs to the front of the room and gets the drum.)

3. *March!* (When teacher puts in the punctuation, George

45

takes the mark as a signal to beat the drum and the pupils begin to move.)

When the pupils have reached their destination George puts the drum away.

The teacher writes, *Thank you, George.*

George says, "You're welcome, Miss—."

II. For morning work.

The teacher writes, *Good morning, children.*

(Pupils rise and say, "Good morning, Miss—.")

The teacher writes, *Please close the door, May.* When May returns teacher has written, *Thank you, May.*

May replies, "You're welcome, Miss—."

III. Just before the books are used in a reading lesson.

The teacher writes, *Please pass the books, James.* Or if a guest comes in, *You may give your book to our guest, Edith.*

IV. Just before dismissing in the afternoon the teacher writes:

Please pass the basket, May.

Thank you, May.

Good night, children.

Pupils rise and say, "Good night, Miss—."

V. When distributing materials, the teacher writes:

1. *Helpers, stand!* (Pupils who are appointed as helpers stand and take materials to be distributed.)

2. *Pass.*

VI. In singing time.

1. *Let's have a concert. You may sing, James.*

2. *Clap.* (Pupils clap when James has finished.)

3. *You may sing, Elizabeth.* When Elizabeth finishes the teacher points to the word *clap.*

Action Lessons

Make the class work lively by originality in the introduction of new devices, in word drill, and in lessons generally, that the exercises may not become monotonous. Require the sentences of the lessons to be acted whenever possible in beginning work.

Sample Lessons in Silent Reading

I. Let us play "The Little Red Hen." You may be the hen, Mary. You may be the pig, Jack. You may be the cat, Alice. You may be the dog, Ben.

II. We are going to play "The Boy and the Goat." You may be the boy, Frank. John, you may be the goat. You may be the rabbit, Bert. Grace may be the squirrel. William may be the fox. Alice, you may be the bee.

There are so many practical uses for silent sentence reading that it is unnecessary to have the children do absurd things just for the sake of having them read and act. For instance, rather than ask a child merely to "Run to the door," write, "Please close the door," or "Please open the door."

Books for Supplementary Reading

Books for supplementary reading should be selected with great care. The teacher should look them through deliberately, asking:

1. Will they be interesting to the children?

2. Will they create in the child a desire to read?

3. Do they lead to consecutive thinking or are they disconnected in thought?

4. Will they enrich the lives of these children?

5. Would the material be considered acceptable reading for children outside of school?

Teaching the Child to Copy or Write the Words

1. Write a known word on the blackboard.

2. Have the class watch you trace the word with a pointer.

3. Have the child hold up his pencil and think of it as long enough to reach the board. Let him trace with the teacher.

4. Pupils trace the form with the pencil in the air without help.

5. Cover up the word. Pupils trace in the air.

6. Ask them if they can think the word. (It is covered.)

7. If they cannot form a mental picture of the word, repeat these steps until they can.

8. When they can see the word mentally, erase the word and let them write from this mental image.

9. Teach other new words in the same way, always requiring the pupil to write from the image.

10. Repeat until the pupil uses the process mechanically for all new and old words.

Drill Upon the Words

1. Reserve a place upon the board to list words as fast as learned.

2. Review the list by skipping about as part of each day's lesson.

3. Place words in all possible combinations and drill until the recognition of words is instantaneous.

SECTION IV

PHONICS

DEFINITIONS OF TERMS USED

A *phonogram* is a letter or character used to represent a particular sound. Phonograms are spoken of as *simple phonograms* and as *blended* or *compound phonograms.*

A *phonogram* represents a single sound. It includes the consonants; the consonant digraphs as ch, sh, wh, th, gh, ph, ng, ck, etc.; the vowels; the diphthongs ow, ou, oy, oi; the vowel digraphs ai, ay, ey, ei, ee, ei, etc.; and the vowel equivalents igh, eigh, etc.

A *sight word* is a word that has been taught as a whole. The word is recognized as a unit from the mental picture which has been formed of it.

Work in phonics is an aid only to provide tools by which the child may gain independence in reading. The more skillful the pupil is in the use of these tools, the more easily will he get the thought and feeling of the author.

The written and printed words a child first meets in learning to read are strange symbols to him. They mean nothing until they are interpreted. This interpretation is, at first, made by the teacher through:

1. Direct association of the object with its written or printed name. For example, she writes the word *seed* on the board and holds the object beside the name. Later she writes the word, and, without speaking the word, asks the pupils to show her what it means. They say nothing, but point to the object or the picture of it.

2. Direct association of action with the phrases or words, written or printed, that suggest it. For example, the teacher writes the word *clap* on the board, and interprets its meaning by clapping her hands instead of by speaking the word.

3. Association of written or printed symbol with the idea represented through the spoken word, a symbol which we

49

suppose the child to understand, since he has heard words spoken for six years. This is the plan especially recommended in this book.

So long as a child depends on his teacher to tell him the words his eye does not at once recognize, just so long he has not learned to read—to get words—and through words, the thought and feeling of the printed page.

For five years at least the child who enters the primary school has acquired words through hearing them spoken. Now he sees these words printed; and since our language is in part spelled phonetically, the knowledge of the sound values of the letters helps a child to find out from the written word the spoken word with which he is already familiar, and for which the written word, in a measure, stands.

To be sure, this finding out for himself each new word is a slower way of getting the thought from a sentence than being told by the teacher or classmate, but, while speed in reading is without doubt an end to be desired and worked for, it is not the first one to be accomplished. It is only by attaining independent power in word-recognition that learners acquire freedom.

How shall we teach the children to use the sound values of the letters as a means of making them independent in reading? The following outline is suggested as one of the many possible ways of getting at the essentials with a small amount of "red tape" and no "padding."

EAR-DRILL

What Shall We Aim at? By the end of the first six months in school we want pupils who meet new words on the pages of their first readers to attack them at once by thinking in order the phonic elements and then blending these elements into the word. But that they may do this, preparation and drill like the following are needed, at first not at all in connection with the reading lesson proper.

Training pupils to be attentive to sound. Tap the bell or a glass with a pencil. Pupils to note the sound. Tap another object. Pupils note the sound. Tap them again. Have pupils note the difference in the sounds. Pupils close their eyes. Teacher taps one or the other of the objects already tapped. Pupils called upon to tell what was sounded. Test with three sounds, with four sounds, with sounds quite similar. Vary exercise by having a pupil do the tapping, other pupils to name the sound.

Slow pronunciation. After the first story is completed, several times each day, the teacher should accustom the ears of the children to hearing words analyzed into their component parts as suggested in the outlined phonic drills. Now that sounds dry, dead and uninteresting, but the actual *doing* of it should be lively, quick, and often even merry. Time and energy are both saved when lively interest reduces the necessity for drill to a minimum.

1. Testing and varying. She writes *red* upon the board, a word they know well. The children pronounce it. She erases *r.* "What has gone?" she asks. "What is left?" Then she writes *b* in the place where *r* stood. "Who can find out the word? Let's sound it and see what it says." Children sound *b-ed* and pronounce *bed*. This drill may begin with the first Series taught and may be rapidly extended as the various Series are brought into use.

2. Dictation. The teacher at another time may dictate to the children, to write for themselves, simple words made up from the elements with which they are very familiar and have them written in the air and on the board many times. These words should not be those they know at sight, or the joy of creating will be lost in the effort to recall a hazy image from memory. Such words as me, no, so, are enough to test the powers of the children at first, and the teacher must speak them slowly and plainly. Each child should do this work correctly, and, after writing from dictation, should go back over his list of words and pronounce it, before the lesson ends, either alone, or in concert with others.

After the first story has been read, these kinds of drill for fixing phonic values in the memory are going on daily, at a time removed from the regular reading lesson, which concerns itself so far with words, sentences and stories. But when the children can read a number of pages from *The Primer* readily, the teacher begins to connect the work in phonics with the reading. A new word is to be taught, in connection with picture, story, or nature lesson, for example the word *rabbit*. "I know," she says, "that you haven't seen me write this word before, but perhaps you can find it out and whisper it to me." And from this point she pushes and leads and guides and encourages the children to find out things for themselves. It needs patience and persistence, but it is well worth the while. Two rules are needed here for the teacher.

a. Very rarely do for the children the thing they can do for themselves.

b. Still more rarely ask them to do a thing they have no preparation for doing.

3. A Guessing game. Here the teacher may introduce a game. "I am thinking of a word I want you to guess. I'll give you a hint. It begins like this," and she gives the sound of the letter *m*. If the children are slow to get the hint and guess at random, she suggests, "It might be *mine, men* or *me*, but it is none of those— yet it begins as they do. Listen!—*m*—" and the children try again.

General Suggestions

Have drills, *bright* and *quick* and *short*, but frequent. Encourage each child to use all the knowledge and power he has in finding out a sentence for himself, but be responsible for furnishing him the needed power and knowledge beforehand.

Do not let children lose what has once been learned, but remember that a thing has not been learned with one or two presentations—often not with many presentations. Do not hesitate to repeat, at first for *accuracy*, to be sure the symbol is associated with the right sound, and then for *speed* in making that association.

Make the children delight in independence, in finding out for themselves, and so find an early joy in reading.

By the time the children have finished *The Primer*, they not only have a considerable list of words recognized at sight, but are not afraid to meet those they have never seen before, for they know they can find them out by the help of phonics and the context of the thought.

Reading should by this time have become a pleasure. The fun of finding out what a page says, and then lingering over and "tasting" the thoughts expressed appeals to all normally constituted children, unless the thought is unworthy, or the habit of independent reading poorly taught from the beginning. *Worthless material destroys the motive and kills the joy of learning to read.*

Kinds of Lessons

1. Study lessons with the teachers in class time.

2. Seat work based upon the story previously read with the teacher.

3. Silent reading based upon vocabulary and thought used in *The Primer*, but changing order of words and sentence.

4. Oral lessons in reading for fluency, natural expression, etc.

5. Lessons for quickening the pace, without mentioning speed to the pupil, in reading familiar material.

This idea of speed in early reading may be misunderstood. The aim is to avoid hesitation and drawling. There is an equal danger that, as pupils gain in freedom, they will fail in grouping, so essential to interpretation and expression.

In all of these, use is made of phonics and word drills, though most emphasis is placed upon the thought content and its expression in sentences.

When children are ready to begin *First Reader* they should have the ability to get many new words phonetically.

By the end of the first grade pupils should have had drills in 80 Phonic Series and should have power to use the phonic knowledge gained.

Explanations of Phonic Drills

Editor's Note: In the following two pages, Treadwell and Free offer a summary of phonic for all ten stories. Putting the information in one place simplifies the process of planning for the teacher. The rule of thumb is that the phonic work follows the telling of the story and during the several days it takes the students to read aloud the story. The exception is the first story, *The Little Red Hen,* in which work with consonants is begun after telling and students reading by sight word rather than during student reading. Phonic drill should be done daily for 2-5 minutes several times a day.

There need be no Phonic Series work with *The Little Red Hen,* but after its completion, the drills with consonant elements should begin and thereafter the Phonic Series lessons should occur daily throughout at least the first two grades.

While reading *The Little Red Hen,* the consonant work should be on *r* in *red, h* in *hen, p* in *pig,* and *l* in *little.*

While the children are reading *The Gingerbread Boy,* the consonant drill is on *n* in *not, d* in *dog, y* in *you,* and *c* in *cat.* Here drill in the Phonic Series may begin, and Series 1 through 4 should be done while reading this story.

With *The Boy and the Goat,* the consonant lessons are with *m* in *man, s* in *so, b* in *but,* and *th* in *then.* At the same time there should be drill in the Phonic Series from 5 to 8, inclusive.

The consonant work while reading *The Pancake* is with *f* in *fox, t* in *to, g* in *get,* and *k* in *kill.* Phonic Series from 9 to 12, inclusive, should receive regular drill.

During the reading of *Chicken Little,* the phonic drill will be with *cr* in *cry, wh* in *why,* and *qu* in *quench.* Add Phonic Series from 13 to 16, inclusive, with reviews of former Series.

The consonant drills with *The Three Billy Goats Gruff* will be with *ch* in *chicken, sn* in *snout,* and *sk* in *sky.* Add to these a thorough review in all Phonic Series already taught.

While reading *Little Tuppens, The Three Bears,* and *Little Spider's First Web,* the consonant work will be with *gr* in *gruff, th* in *thank,* and *tr* in *trip.* Complete the Series from 17 to 20 inclusive, and give a thorough review of all previous phonic drills, including the Phonic Series to 20. When this is done, the consonant elements will have been mastered. It will be noticed that the consonant elements are taught from words that have been taught in a former story. When *The Primer* is completed, there should have been thorough drill, also on twenty of the Phonic Series.

Let it be remembered that these phonic drills should be short but frequent. In some schools these drills are given for from two to five minutes at a time, two or three times a day, conditions varying with the size of the class and the time at the disposal of the teacher. The phonic work, whether the teacher uses the book in the beginning or later, should be given as indicated.

The phonic lessons to be given with the work of *First Reader* should cover 59 additional Phonic Series, making 79 in all to the end of the first year.

The remaining 121 Series involve more difficulty and may require more careful drill. If they are not completed by the end of the second year, they may go over into third year work. But most teachers will experience little difficulty in including all of them in the second year's work.

Arrangement of the Phonic Series

In the Series from 1 to 32, inclusive, the short sounds of the vowels are taught. No consonant is at any time required which has not been already taught from sight words.

Next come the Series teaching the long sounds of the vowels. These include series 33 to 61.

In the reviews of these Series it will be noticed that the first word of each Series is used. All the words of the reviews are given as wholes and, in the review drills, no word should be separated into its elements, unless pupils fail to recognize it as a whole.

In the first 32 Series it should be observed that when a vowel is followed by a single consonant, the vowel has the short sound. This may be shown to children but, in no case should this or any other rule be taught formally in the first two years. It may be suggested here that, because our language is not phonetic, few rules can be made to which there may not be exceptions. But the rules herein suggested are sufficiently general in their application to afford great aid in word mastery. The exceptions to the rules, in most cases, may well await the greater maturity of children.

In teaching the long vowels, it may be shown that, if two vowels have a single consonant between them the first vowel is long and the final vowel is silent.

In all of the Series through 79 the soft sound of *s* is used, but in Series 80 is introduced the hard or *z* sound of this element.

From Series 62 to 79 two consonants follow one vowel. When these two letters have the same sound, like *ck* in Series 62 to 66, or are the same letter doubled, as in Series 67 and 68, only one is sounded.

In Series 81, blended consonants are introduced. A few of these have been used in previous drills, but they have heretofore occurred in sight words—words already known to the children. These blends are used first, as initial phonograms and then as final phonograms.

In Series 86 may be shown that *t* is silent before *ch*. From Series 95 to 120, other consonant combinations are used both as initial and final phonograms. In all of these exercises, the pupils should be practiced in blending so that the consonants blended may form a single sound.

Series 121 to 123 introduces the three sounds of *y*.

In Series 124 to 128, inclusive, *ai* and *ay* are shown to equal long *a*; and from this time forward, other equivalents are used in the Series. Not all equivalents are here used, but it is believed that those omitted, for the most part, will offer little difficulty after a thorough drill with those here given. In some of the equivalents not here given as well as in some of the peculiar and difficult sounds of certain vowels, a discrimination is required that is beyond the ability of children in first and second grades.

From Series 129 to 138, *ea* equals long *e*. From 139 to 145 *ee* equals long *e*. In 146, *ie* equals long *i*. From 147 to 151, *oa* equals long *o*, and 153 shows *ue* equal to long *u*

In 154 and 155, *i* is long when followed by *ld*, *nd*, or *gh*. Series 156 to 157 show *o* long in some other combinations. Series 158 to 160 give drills with *ow*, and from 161 to 166, *ou* is shown to equal *ow*, in 167 *ow* is equal to long *o*, and in 168 *ou* is equal to long *o*.

In Series 169, final *er* is shown. This list may be used, also, to show plurals by adding *s*. Series 170 and 171 use the *ing* termination.

In 172, *gn* equals *n*; in 173, *kn* equals *n*; in 174, *wr* equals *r*; in 175, *gu* equals *g*; in 176, *bu* equals *b*; in 177, *bt* equals *t*, and 178 shows *mb* equal to *m*.

Series 179 through 181 show that when one consonant is used between two vowels, the first vowel is long, and that when two consonants are so used, the first vowel is short.

From Series 182 to 200 are taught the following equivalents: *ea* equals short *e*, *ea* equals long *a*, *ed* equals *t*, *ei* equals long *a*, *ie* equals long *e*, *eigh* equals long *a*, *ey* equals long *a*. Also *oo* is taught in both values, *u* is equal to *oo* short, *oi* equals *oy*, *c* is equal to soft *s* when used before *i*, *e* and *y*, *g* equals *j* before *e*, *i* and *y*, *dg* equals *j*, *ph* equals *f* and *gh* equals *f*.

PHONIC SERIES

1	6	10	14	17
r ed	s ob	w ill	m et	t in
b ed	b ob	t ill	s et	s in
f ed	r ob	b ill	g et	b in
l ed	c ob	s ill	b et	f in
N ed	f ob	f ill	l et	d in
	j ob	r ill	j et	p in
2	m ob	k ill	n et	k in
h en		h ill	p et	
d en	**7**	m ill		**18**
p en	p ig	p ill	**15**	p up
m en	b ig		r un	c up
B en	r ig	**11**	d un	s up
	d ig	d og	s un	
3	j ig	b og	n un	**19**
c at	w ig	h og	g un	r ap
f at		c og	b un	c ap
h at	**8**	f og	f un	g ap
r at	ox	j og		l ap
m at	b ox		**16**	n ap
s at	f ox	**12**	f ed	t ap
		c ut	g ot	m ap
4	**9**	n ut	t an	s ap
c an	it	r ut	h at	
D an	w it	b ut	s at	**20**
f an	s it	h ut	b at	p ad
r an	b it		t en	b ad
p an	p it	**13**	l ed	l ad
	f it	d id		s ad
5	h it	l id		m ad
n ot	m it	b id		h ad
d ot		k id		f ad
g ot		h id		g ad
c ot				
p ot				
j ot				
h ot				

21	27	Review	33	37
l eg	r ag	red	b e	g o
p eg	w ag	hen	m e	s o
b eg	b ag	cat	h e	n o
k eg	t ag	can	th e	
	s ag	not	sh e	**38**
22		sob	w e	b ite
l ip	**28**	pig		k ite
t ip	ax	ox	**34**	s ite
d ip	t ax	it	m ake	m ite
r ip	w ax	will	b ake	
h ip		dog	sh ake	**39**
s ip	**29**	cut	c ake	g oat
n ip	c ab	did	t ake	m oat
	t ab	met	f ake	c oat
23		run	r ake	fl oat
m ud	**30**	tin	m ake	b oat
b ud	h im	pup	s ake	
	d im	rap	l ake	**40**
24	r im	pad		c ane
b ug		leg	**35**	p ane
r ug	**31**	lip	b ee	m ane
d ug	f ix	mud	f ee	
p ug	s ix	bug	s ee	**41**
m ug	m ix	tub	l ee	ate
h ug		am	tr ee	d ate
t ug	**32**	rag		r ate
	r od	ax	**36**	f ate
25	G od	cab	t old	m ate
t ub	p od	him	c old	g ate
h ub	h od	fix	b old	l ate
r ub	s od	rod	h old	h ate
	n od		g old	
26			f old	
am			s old	
S am			m old	
h am				
j am				

59

42

s ame
t ame
c ame
n ame
f ame
l ame
g ame

43

c ape
t ape

44

m ade
w ade
f ade

45

h ide
w ide
b ide
t ide
r ide
s ide

46

d ime
t ime
l ime

47

f ine
p ine
d ine
n ine
w ine
f ine
l ine

48

r ode
c ode
m ode

49

n ote
c ote
d ote
m ote
r ote

50

g ale
p ale
s ale
t ale

51

p ole
m ole
h ole
s ole

52

t une
J une
pr une
r ule
r ude

53

p ure
c ure

54

m ule
m ute

55

c ore
t ore
s ore
m ore
w ore

56

l ope
c ope
d ope
r ope
m ope
h ope

57

r age
p age
c age
s age

58

b ase
c ase
v ase

59

c ave
w ave
g ave
s ave
p ave

60

m ile
t ile
p ile
f ile

61

f ire
w ire
h ire
t ire

Review

be
make
bee
told
go
bite
goat
cane
ate
same
cape
made
hide
dime
fine
rode
note
gale
pole
tune
pure
mule
core
lope
rage
base
cave
mile
fire

62

b ack
l ack
p ack
t ack
s ack

63

n eck
d eck

64

s ick
k ick
t ick
l ick
p ick

65

r ock
l ock

66

d uck
l uck
b uck

67

s ell
N ell
t ell
b ell
w ell
f ell

68	**74**	**Review**	**82**	**86**
p uff	f ist	(cont.)	cr y	D utch
r uff	m ist	sell	cr ape	b otch
c uff	l ist	puff	cr ew	n otch
b uff		and	cr ime	p itch
m uff	**75**	end	cr ate	w itch
	r ust	bent	cr ow	d itch
69	m ust	tint	cr umb	h itch
and	j ust	rest		c atch
h and	d ust	fist	**83**	m atch
s and		rust	gr and	p atch
l and	**76**	camp	gr ave	l atch
b and	c amp	bump	gr ip	h atch
	l amp	felt	gr ill	
70	d amp	gift	gr it	**87**
end			gr in	m uch
m end	**77**	**80**	gr ow	s uch
b end	b ump	is	gr ew	r ich
s end	p ump	h is	gr een	
	j ump	as	gr ound	**88**
71	d ump	h as		sh ape
b ent	l ump	p ins	**84**	sh am
s ent		r ugs	ch ick	sh ell
r ent	**78**	r ose	ch oke	sh elf
w ent	f elt	r ise	ch op	sh ed
t ent	b elt	n ose	ch at	sh ip
	w elt	w ise	ch in	sh ine
72	m elt		ch ase	sh un
t int		**81**	ch ill	sh ut
h int	**79**	wh en	ch ap	sh ot
m int	g ift	wh at	ch afe	sh one
l int	s ift	wh ile		sh ore
	l ift	wh o	**85**	sh ave
73		wh ite	p un ch	sh all
r est	**Review**	wh ole	b en ch	sh ade
v est	back	wh ine	b un ch	sh ake
t est	neck	wh ich	l un ch	
w est	sick	wh ere		
b est	rock	wh ip		
n est	duck			

61

89	94	96	100	103
ash	thr ob	cl od	sp an	scr ap
s ash	thr ift	cl ose	sp ade	scr ub
d ash	thr ill	cl ove	sp in	scr ape
l ash	thr one	cl ock	sp end	scr atch
c ash	thr ash	cl am	sp ill	
m ash	thr ush	cl ap	sp ell	**104**
f ish	thr ive	cl ick	sp ine	sc ore
d ish	thr ust	cl uck	sp ot	sc um
w ish		cl ip	sp oke	sc at
r ush	**Review**	cl ub	sp un	sc amp
	is		sp ite	sc ale
90	when	**97**	sp ike	Sc otch
th ick	cry	fl at	sp ire	
th in	grand	fl ag		**105**
th ump	chick	fl ake	**101**	sk in
	punch	fl ame	br ag	sk im
91	Dutch	fl ash	br an	sk ip
w id th	much	fl ock	br ake	sk iff
t en th	shape	fl op	br ave	sk ill
	ash	fl it	br im	sk ull
92	thick	fl ax	br ick	sk ate
th e	tenth		br ide	sk etch
th en	width	**98**	br ine	
th em	the	gl ad	br oke	**106**
th an	bathe	gl ide	br ush	r isk
th at	throb	gl aze		br isk
th us		gl obe	**102**	t usk
th ese	**95**		cr ab	d usk
th ose	bl ed	**99**	cr ib	h usk
th is	bl ade	pl an	cr ock	m usk
th ine	bl ack	pl ant	cr ack	
	bl ess	pl ate	cr ate	**107**
93	bl ame	pl ush	cr ane	dr op
b athe	bl ot	pl ume	cr amp	dr ag
w ith	bl ock	pl um	cr imp	dr ug
	bl aze	pl ot	cr op	dr ip
	bl unt		cr ust	dr ill
	bl ush		cr ush	dr ift
			cr ept	dr ive

107 (cont.)	110 (cont.)	113	118	Review (cont.)
dr ove	tr od	t aste	sw am	print
dr one	tr uck	p aste	sw im	trap
dr ape		b aste	sw um	strap
dr ess	**111**	w aste	sw ept	stab
dr um	str ap		sw ift	taste
	str ip	**114**	sw ine	lest
108	str ipe	l est		trust
fr et	str ive	cr est	**119**	smell
fr esh	str ict	ch est	tw ist	snap
Fr ench	str ike	bl est	tw ins	swam
fr ill	str ide		tw ine	twist
fr isk	str oke	**115**	tw ig	quench
fr og	str etch	tr ust	tw itch	
fr om		cr ust		**121**
fr oze	**112**	r ust	**120**	y es
fr ame	st ab		qu ench	y et
fr ock	st ep	**116**	qu ick	y ell
	st em	sm ell	qu ack	
109	st ack	sm elt	qu it	**122**
pr int	st and	sm ile	qu ite	H en ny
pr ide	st ate	sm ith	qu ill	m er ry
pr ize	st ump	sm ash	qu ilt	c an dy
pr op	st ale	sm ack		k it ty
pr ose	st ake	sm oke	**Review**	p en ny
pr ess	st iff		bled	s un ny
	st ilt	**117**	clod	f un ny
110	st ill	sn ap	flat	c ar ry
tr ap	st ick	sn ag	glad	j ol ly
tr act	st one	sn ug	plan	
tr ack	st ove	sn ake	span	**123**
tr ash	st op	sn uff	brag	cr y
tr amp	st itch	sn iff	crab	m y
tr ade	st ub	sn ipe	scrap	dr y
tr ip	st uck	sn are	score	sl y
tr im	st uff		skin	sp y
tr ill	st ore		risk	sk y
tr ick	st ole		drop	sh y
tr ot	st ump		fret	fl y
				wh y
				th y

63

124	129	135	141	146
aid	t ea	t ear	f eel	d ie
p aid	s ea	n ear	h eel	t ie
br aid	p ea	h ear	p eel	h ie
m aid	**130**	cl ear	r eel	l ie
125	each	**136**	st eel	**147**
ail	p each	east	**142**	t oad
p ail	r each	b east	s een	l oad
h ail	t each	f east	k een	r oad
f ail	**131**	**137**	gr een	**148**
n ail	w eak	eat	qu een	oak
r ail	l eak	m eat	**143**	s oak
s ail	p eak	b eat	k eep	cl oak
b ail	sp eak	n eat	st eep	**149**
126	str eak	s eat	d eep	oat
aim	sn eak	h eat	p eep	g oat
m aim	squ eak	**138**	sh eep	c oat
cl aim	**132**	pl ea se	sl eep	fl oat
127	h eal	t ea se	cr eep	thr oat
r ain	s eal	ea sy	sw eep	**150**
tr ain	st eal	**139**	**144**	t oast
br ain	m eal	s eed	f eet	r oast
gr ain	squ eal	f eed	m eet	c oast
str ain	**133**	n eed	b eet	b oast
p ain	dr eam	d eed	sw eet	**151**
pl ain	t eam	w eed	gr eet	oar
ch ain	str eam	bl eed	str eet	r oar
128	st eam	**140**	**145**	s oar
h ay	**134**	w eek	fr eeze	h oar se
p ay	b ean	ch eek	sn eeze	c oar se
s ay	m ean	cr eek	br eeze	b oar d
w ay	l ean		squ eeze	
m ay	cl ean			
pl ay				
st ay				
str ay				
pr ay				

152	**157**	**161**	**167**	**169**
t oe	r oll	ouch	l ow	(cont.)
f oe	t oll	p ouch	fl ow	rocker
w oe	tr oll	c ouch	gl ow	painter
h oe	str oll	sl ouch	b ow	summer
	p ost		bl ow	
153	m ost	**162**	r ow	**170**
d ue	b olt	l oud	gr ow	s ing
c ue	j olt	pr oud	cr ow	k ing
h ue	c olt	cl oud	m ow	r ing
s ue	b oth		sn ow	str ing
	f orth	**163**	sh ow	sl ing
154	p ork	f ound	thr ow	w ing
w ild	p orch	p ound	b owl	sw ing
ch ild		r ound	own	th ing
b ind	**158**	gr ound	s own	br ing
bl ind	c ow	m ound	m own	
gr ind	n ow	b ound	bl own	**171**
m ind	b ow	s ound	fl own	jump ing
k ind	h ow	w ound	gr own	rest ing
f ind	r ow			runn ing
	pl ow	**164**	**168**	rubb ing
155	m ow	our	f our	help ing
s igh		s our	c our t	add ing
s igh t	**159**	fl our	c our se	wish ing
r igh t	owl		p our	swing ing
bright t	h owl	**165**		try ing
fl igh t	gr owl	m ouse	**169**	play ing
f igh t	f owl	h ouse	flower	read ing
m igh t		bl ouse	winter	
t igh t	**160**		sister	**Review**
n igh t	t own	**166**	rubber	yes
	d own	out	better	Henny
156	g own	p out	timber	cry
old	dr own	sp out	pitcher	aid
h old	br own	tr out	deeper	ail
g old	cr own	st out	hammer	aim
c old		sh out	older	rain
sc old		s outh	colder	hay
m old		m outh	dinner	each
s old				weak

Review	173	178	Review	185
(cont.)	kn it	(cont.)	gnat	(cont.)
heal	kn ife	th umb	knit	packed
dream	kn ight	pl umb	wren	milked
bean	kn ot	l amb	guide	puffed
tear	kn ob		buy	
east	kn ee	**179**	debt	**186**
please	kn eel	holy	limb	v eil
freeze	kn ow	holly	holy	v ein
die	kn ack	later	silver	r ein
toad	kn ock	latter	hero	sk ein
oak		filing		
oat	**174**	filling	**182**	**187**
toast	wr en	pining	h ead	gr ief
oar	wr ench	pinning	r ead	th ief
toe	wr eck	mating	tr ead	ch ief
due	wr ap	matting	br ead	br ief
wild	wr ite	summer	d eaf	y ield
sigh	wr ing	carry	m eant	sh ield
right	wr ist		sw eat	
old		**180**	w ealth	**188**
roll	**175**	sil ver		eight
cow	gu ide	vel vet	**183**	fr eight
owl	gu est	win dow	gr eat	w eight
town	gu ess	sis ter	st eak	w eigh
pouch	ro gue	pic nic	br eak	sl eigh
loud	pla gue			r eign
found		**181**	**184**	
sour	**176**	he ro	tint ed	**189**
mouse	bu y	sto ry	jolt ed	th ey
pout	bu ild	ba ker	seat ed	pr ey
low		mu sic	wick ed	wh ey
four	**177**	du ty	grad ed	
flower	de bt	ze ro	coast ed	**190**
jumping	dou bt	pa per	mend ed	roared
		gra vy		prayed
172	**178**		**185**	snowed
gn at	li mb		baked	cleaned
gn ash	co mb		ticked	soured
si gn	nu mb		choked	crowed
			liked	

191	**195**	**198**	**Review**
t oo	oil	edge	head
t ool	b oil	hedge	great
r oof	s oil	pledge	tinted
pr oof	t oil	ridge	baked
st ool	c oin	bridge	veil
f ood	j oin	dodge	grief
l oose	n oise	lodge	eight
g oose		judge	they
sh oot	**196**		roared
ch oose	ice	**199**	too
	nice	ph onics	grew
192	price	or phan	good
gr ew	lace	sul phur	put
fl ew	face	ci pher	oil
thr ew	race	ele phant	ice
cr ew	fence	al phabet	age
dr ew	since		edge
	piece	**200**	phonics
193	niece	r ough	rough
g ood	voice	t ough	
h ood	city	l augh	
st ood	spicy	c ough	
h ook	juicy	tr ough	
w ool			
l ook	**197**		
	age		
194	rage		
p ut	sage		
p ull	page		
p uss	cage		
p ush	range		
f ull	danger		
b ush	manger		

Folk Tales

Origins and Transmission

The Primer offers nine folk tales; *First Reader*, thirteen; and *Second Reader*, eight or ten more. It might be well to inquire immediately, therefore, what folk tales are, and why they appeal to all children and to grown persons likewise. As the prefaces to the Readers assert, these folk tales here given are the literary products of many minds, and have survived the centuries. It is a mistake, however, to believe that the making and transmission of folk tales is a process only of the past. Wherever mothers or nurses or teachers tell and retell stories to children, folk tales are growing up, expanding, changing.

Of universal interest. There is today a science of folklore. Great scholars study the simple stories of the people as they study other evidences of past belief and present custom; for what has amused mankind continuously for long periods, they argue, must have in it the essence of man's thinking. The growth and dissemination of folk stories is a phenomenon of importance. The popularity of the narratives is no more a fact of the past than eating is. The form of what we eat and the way we eat it may have changed from time to time, but the elemental food-stuffs remain the same. Man's nature craves them, and when it gets them they prove satisfying. We need not be surprised that the natural man, the child, and the jaded epicure alike find folk stories pleasing. They are elemental food. But not to carry the figure too far, and simply bearing in mind the fact brought out by it, let us go back to inquire what a folk tale really is, and along with general impressions gather a few specific distinctions. Since a science of folklore exists, for a student who wishes to understand these stories, there is a nomenclature to be learned, a set of definitions to be borne in mind, a history to be glanced at, some great names to be remembered.

What are folk tales? A folk tale is a story that grows up among a people, or folk, around an idea either originated or adopted by the folk. The earliest form is always of an oral nature if not actually oral, and its usual transmission—a far more important fact than source—is oral. Today, despite our many books and newspapers, folk tales circulate orally. Our favorite narratives we seldom if ever saw in print when we were children, although they were in print no doubt before we were born. Our mothers, or nurses, or big sisters, or teachers, told us the stories first, even if we read them later. The delight of the reading was no less but greater because of the familiarity. The phrases on the pages seemed to be of the very structure of our thinking. Hence the delight.

How they grow. It is said that a folk story "grows up" because no one seems to know who first starts such a narrative on its way, or because the later versions because of oral repetitions vary among themselves and are each different from the earlier, and because the story represents common folk thinking. Right here it might be well to preclude confusion. Everyone recognizes a possible double meaning in the word "folk tale"; namely, that of "tale composed by the folk" or simply that of "tale told among the folk," even though it may have been originally a translation or importation.

The distinction may have a meaning and it may not. If the first definition is understood to imply that a whole folk instantly and collectively composes a piece of literature without the intervention of individuals, the definition becomes nonsense. Or if it is understood to imply that a piece composed by one man or one woman or one child might not become loved by the folk as a whole, taken to their hearts, told and retold among them, become a part of their household thinking—in other words, might not become to them and through them a real folk tale— then, too, the distinction is nonsense. In fact, all that is needed is time. It is because the world has forgotten the authors of our best folk tales that we cannot mention them. Because we can mention Perrault, however, our common version of Cinderella is no less a folk tale. That the process of story-making was any different in the days of Rameses II from what it is now, except for the facility of reproduction and transmission, a thinking man cannot believe. Human nature has not so changed in three thousand years. We have but to look about us to know the folk story process. We have but to read history to verify our understanding of it.

Length of life. But when we look about us we must
remember that the process we are investigating is essentially
an oral process, that the stories we are investigating are living
things that change so long as they live. When they have ceased
to change, they have ceased to live as folk stories. Some may
linger on, perhaps, as grim ghosts of departed literature or be
found on shelves as mummies of antiquity. But actually a good
folk tale is both as eternal and as changeable as the folk that
tells it; indeed, an excellent story always overpasses locality
and country—even more than a virile folk overpasses. For this
reason, if for no other, children have a right to hear and to read
folk tales; most of them are a rich heritage and an everlasting
possession. The rude common sense as well as the nonsense of
the ancients and the moderns is stored in them.

How originated. Any set of events, actual or imaginary,
occurring anywhere, may become a folk story after undergoing
the folk story process. The immediate handing down is very
simple. It is easily explained by a household fact. A new mother
naturally tells the favorite narrative her mother told her when
she was a child. The stories pass on down the generations, and
become in time traditional, current among a large family, a
village, perhaps a whole folk finally. When the narrator has
a larger audience than immediate kin, the diffusion is much
faster. If the new mother came from a neighboring or a foreign
people, how the stream of family tradition is enriched! The word
"tradition" is a simple word and does not necessarily belong to
scholars. Any particular story, belief, or usage handed down
becomes a tradition.

Link ages and people. A number of folk stories, like the
Cinderella and the Sleeping Beauty narratives, have lived
longer than the races that now cherish them. "It is certain," says
Andrew Lang, "that the best-known popular tales were current
in Egypt under Rameses II, and that many of them were known
to Homer, and are introduced or alluded to in the *Odyssey*."
This is a lovely thought, because it makes the solidarity of the
human race a more vivid fact. The small child in the classroom
in America today, with perfect confidence, puts his hand into
the brown palm of the great king of Egypt, and enjoys with him
the old, old stories—stories no doubt old to his people then, a
thousand years or more before the Christian era.

It is essential to folk tale that the appeal be universal, although national peculiarities are apparent in the versions. Sainte-Beuve has reminded us that had we inherited no such tales, and had we started to tell stories in the nursery in full civilization, the incidents of *Puss in Boots* would not have been invented. Sainte-Beuve is right, but he has reminded us only of the fact that folk stories are made out of known elements or similar elements. So is everything else.

Place of origin uncertain. The idea of the persistence of the same story has proved extremely fascinating to scholars. It has called out a long line of inquirers, who have kept themselves busy for a century at least. There is nothing very mysterious about the matter, however, but just something materially difficult—the discovery of reliable records and evidence. Indications there are a-plenty, but proofs that this locality instead of that gave rise to a particular story are hard to find. And that one locality and only one was the cradle of all marchen, or popular tales, is a still harder thesis, as its advocates have learned by reason of their many doughty opponents. When we know where the first acorn or the first oak tree came from, perhaps we can answer the question as to where the first folk tale, or the first version of a given folk tale, originated. Until the scholars have brought that time about, we must content ourselves with the knowledge that individualized versions spring up and flourish for a century or two and then die, or lose their identity, but that the form and general content of folk tales go on forever.

Variation. A common condition connected with the oral transmission of even our best-established stories is variation. Minute particulars are seldom transmitted orally. They are left out or created spontaneously under local inspiration. Only the large central events that make one tale recognizable as itself and not another, remain the same. And sometimes even the events change and shift and nothing but the motif, or central idea, stays fixed. The simplicity of the versions of the folk tales in primers and first readers is consequent upon this fact of the adaptability to audiences. On the other hand—and here is a psychological truth that all good narrators take advantage of—striking and charming peculiarities of style or utterance often persist even though they may be connected with only minor details. Mothers and teachers know how the big voice or the little voice at the expected place in an oral narrative is demanded by the experienced listener, and how the occurrence of the emphasis favorite with other children seldom fails to delight the novice. Crude rhythm, rhymes, and repetition of situation are all aids to oral delivery, and in our ancient stories are evidence of it. They are aids both to the narrator and to the listener. They make memory easy on the part of the one and attention easy on the part of the other. Repetition of situation permits extension also, which is a delight to both the narrator and the listener when a good folk tale is going. Hence often the end of one story is added to that of another.

Before we look at the stories themselves and assort them to their types, we should note at some length how they were got together and who it was that did the work.

Charles Perrault (1628-1703)

Charles Perrault, a Frenchman, was one of the first of the moderns to create an art interest in folk tales; and he created it by the very simple process of retelling the stories. He presented to the public (1694-1697), in charming and simple prose form, eight household narratives taken down from oral recitation. He sent them first as contributions to a small magazine published at The Hague, called Moetjen's *Recueil* (Miscellany), then later put them out as a book bearing his son's name, Perrault Dermancour.

In the hall of fame. At the time that he began to publish the stories of the people, Charles Perrault was a member of the royal academy under Louis xiv, and was the noted hero of the great Battle of the Books, which the critics had been waging for ten years over a remark of Perrault's in a poem read by him before the Academy in 1684. As a result of the poem and the controversy, Perrault had become recognized as the champion of the moderns; and Boileau, properly enough, the champion of the ancients. Perrault in his poem entitled *The Age of Louis xiv* had found fault with the *Odyssey* for containing "old wives' fables," and had said that Homer would have written better had he had the good fortune to be born under Louis xiv. Boileau

had angrily declared Perrault's poem an insult to the great
men of past times, and had begun taking revenge in their name
by writing epigrams on Perrault. Thus the war continued and
spread to other countries. Some members of the Academy took
Boileau's side in the controversy, some Perrault's. Racine, mild
man that he was, pretended not to think Perrault in earnest; but
Perrault continued to uphold his arguments, and to make fun
of persons who think it a fine thing "to publish old books with
a great many notes." In the crisis of the controversy Perrault
wrote what he imagined would be his monument of immortality,
The Comparison of the Ancients and the Moderns (1688-1694)
and *Eulogies of Illustrious Men of the Age of Louis xiv* (1703).
But these have not proved to be his monument. Men do not
today read lengthy, argumentative poems on the foolish subject
of which is better, the moderns or the ancients; but all the world
reads Perrault's versions of traditional popular stories, his
"Mother Goose's Tales."

Old tales made new. These stories are usually called
"fairy tales," though Perrault did not call them fairy tales, but
"Stories, or Tales of Past Time." And that is what they are, as
we shall see—folk nursery sagas. Perrault felt the common
folk tone of the pieces, and acknowledged it and defended it,
although he did not realize the great antiquity of what he was
retelling or the ultimate significance of the preservation. He
told the stories as current, oral literature coming down from the
past. It is interesting to note that the Recueil advertised itself as
a repository, or miscellany, of "pieces curious and new." The oral
tales of the peasants would be curious and new to the affected
literary world of Louis xiv's day.

Twenty years before Perrault began to write down the oral
narratives of the people, fairy stories and naïve literature in
general had become popular at the court, although only in oral
form; but the popularity was rather a fad than a revival of real
simplicity, and it was in no sense a pledge of scientific interest
in the life of the populace.

Perrault's part in the world. But Perrault's stories ring
true, as the real product of the peasantry of France and of
past ages of peasantry in other lands. The elements are older
than France, older than French civilization as we think of it.

Though these stories manifestly have other civilizations besides
the French reflected in them, they are, however, in Perrault's
versions truly French as well as truly human. How did the
result come about? Simply enough. Perrault took the narratives,
not out of his own imagination, but directly out of the mouth
of the people through the mouth of a child. Perrault's little son
repeated them as the peasant nurse had told them; and Perrault
the father wrote them down, or his son wrote them down in a
more or less crude, natural form, and Perrault edited them.
This conclusion seems to be the best judgment of the critics as
to what part Perrault and as to what part his son had in the
composition; for the eight prose tales edited in book form, as we
have said, were attributed to the son, Perrault Darmancour—
although Perrault, the father, the noted academician, when
they were attacked, defended them and acknowledged a share
in the writing. Contemporaneous criticism seems to establish
the probability that the stories were written down or recited by
the boy as exercises in composition. Perrault was well known
to be interested intelligently in the education of his children,
and to give a good deal of his time to directing it personally.
He fostered ingenuity and originality. He called the process of
putting into acceptable literary form the stories of the nursery
and of the French peasant households "original composition" on
the part of his children. It was original in the truest and most
valuable sense. When the little boy and his father began, few or
none such tales had been written out in French, at least no in
that age. The father rightly thought the work more contributive
than the frivolous redoing of the Greek and Roman classics
which occupied the school children of the day. The Perrault
family believe in things "curious and new."

It is beautiful to think, though, that this jolly,
companionable, modern father, the famous hero of the Battle of
the Books, finally, in spite of himself, and in plan contradiction
to his supposed position, was meeting Homer on his own ground
as a teller of "old wives' fables." It is also satisfying to know
that what created such a storm in Perrault's day is accepted as
an obvious fact now—namely, that the great epics of Homer, in
their elements, first belonged to the people.

The motive. Perrault's stories will live forever as well

as Homer's. The delightful blending of age and youth in them
makes them more valuable than they were before. Perrault
was himself, despite his luck and elevation, essentially a man
of the people. His impatience with scholarship, his breezy and
unblushing amateurism in everything, prove the fact, as well as
does his innate sympathy with the folk of his country. Perrault
is to be remembered for his love of little children and of the
common people shown in a practical way, also, when he was
retiring from his service as minister to the king. It was proposed
that the Tuilleries gardens should be closed to the public and
reserved for royalty only. Perrault protested in the name of little
French children and of common mothers and fathers and nurses,
saying, "I am persuaded that the gardens of the kings are made
so great and spacious that all their children may walk in them."
It was decreed that the gardens should be kept open in the
interest of children forever.

The list. Perrault published three verse tales as well as
the eight prose tales. The prose versions, as we have said, will
always live. They have passed over the boundaries of city and
country and become native in England and America as well as
in France. One has but to give a list to prove the contention
instantly, with a single exception. Here is the list: La Belle
au Bois Dormant (The Sleeping Beauty), Le Petit Chaperon
Rouge (Little Red Riding Hood), La Barbe Bleue (Blue Beard),
Le Maistre Chat, ou Le Chat Botte (Puss in Boots), Les Fees
(Toads and Diamonds), Cendrillon, ou la petite pantoufle de
verre (Cinderella), Riquet a la Houppe (Riquet of the Tuft—not
popular in English), and Le Petit Poucet (Hop o' My Thumb).
These tales received in England the title of "Mother Goose's
Tales" because on all the English chap-books, with various slight
alterations, the frontispiece of the 1697 French edition persisted.
It represents an old woman spinning, and telling tales to a man,
a girl, a little boy, and a cat with a broad grin on its face; and
announces on a placard

> Contes
> Dema
> Mere
> Loye

that is, "Mother Goose's Tales."

THE BROTHERS GRIMM
Jacob Ludwig Carl (1785-1863)
Wilhelm Carl (1786-1859)

The founders of the science of folklore were the brothers Jacob and William Grimm, who published, in 1812-1815, their *Children and Household Tales*, a collection of popular tales taken for the most part directly from the mouths of the common people of Germany.

The mutual friendship of these brothers was in itself fundamental and folk-like. Its simplicity and devotion have passed into a proverb. While their name stands for what is highest and best in German scholarship, it stands also for what is loveliest in human nature—kindliness, industry, enthusiasm, patience, and brotherly love, in both the restricted and universal sense.

Live and work together. Jacob and William Grimm were born one year apart, 1785, 1786. They attended school together, worked together, lived together for seventy-two years, with the exception of one year when William, the younger, was ill, and his brother Jacob went up to the University of Marburg a few months in advance in 1802. William followed, however, in 1803. As boys they had gone through the public school of Cassel together. When William was married, Jacob continued to live with him; and it is said that the children of the family loved their uncle almost as much as they loved their father, and recognized little difference between the two. As men in the world, Jacob and William were brother librarians, brother professors, brother sufferers in the cause of constitutional liberty. When Jacob was professor and librarian at Gottengen and William was under-librarian, they signed, with five other members of the faculty of the university, a protest against the King of Hanover's abrogation of the Constitution he had given to his people a few years before. In punishment the brothers Grimm were dismissed, and went back to Cassel, where they remained without an appointment for three years.

In 1840, however, at the invitation of the King of Prussia, they both accepted professorships in the University of Berlin and membership in the Academy of Science. Jacob lived five years longer than William, but always in the halo of their past companionship. The greatest sorrow that ever came to Jacob's heart was the loss of his brother. He paid a noble and touching tribute to William in a review of his life in an address before the Academy—a pathetic address in which the speaker broke down and cried.

Nature of their work. The brothers Grimm did more than Perrault in that they not only told the stories of the past simply and well, but created a love in the minds of other persons for the simple folk products of all nations and created a reverence for race literature just as it is found. They went at the work of preservation in the spirit of science. For instance, they would collect variants of a story and then, comparing the variants with the best straightforward version they had, they would decide, through their knowledge of the dialects and of anthropology in general, what was probably the ancient and most natural form or the best evolved form. This they would put into the body of their book and would offer the remainder in the notes and the discussion. Some stories, they took from manuscript and other collections, and commented on the source.

ASBJØRNSEN AND MOE

Peter Christen Asbjørnsen (1812-1885) and Jørgen Engebretsen Moe (1813-1882)

Like the Grimm Brothers, Peter Christen Asbjørnsen (1812-1885) and Jørgen Engebretsen Moe (1813-1882) have come down in literary fame together. They met when one was fourteen and the other was thirteen years old, and remained fast friends the rest of their lives. Each one, inspired by the work of the German collectors, determined to write down for preservation whatever Norse folk tales he should come across from day to day. After working a year or more alone, the young men decided, in 1834, to do the final revision and the editing and publishing together. It happened, or came as a result of their association, that they had practically the same way of thinking and the same vigorous and charming narrative style. The partnership was extremely fortunate. It resulted in one of the best books of Norwegian literature, and altogether one of the best folk story collections in the world. These narratives, even when retold in the simplest form for young readers, retain the crispness of northern thought and expression.

How they gathered stories. Asbjørnsen, who became zoologist and spent much of his time investigating for the university in the way of his profession along the coasts of Norway, collected many of his stories meanwhile, especially from the west coast and the Hardanger fjord; and Moe, who became a clergyman, searched in the southern mountains and the remote districts as his duties and holidays permitted.

The first volume came out in 1842-1843 under the title *Norse Folk Tales,* and the second volume in 1844. These two volumes were received with acclaim, and have been deservedly popular ever since. Dr. George Webbe Dasent began translating them into English almost immediately, and after fifteen years published a first edition in Edinburg called "Popular Tales from the Norse." This volume lacked thirteen of the Norse stories, but contained a long preface by Dasent on the Origin and Diffusion of Popular Literature. Later, in a second edition, the preface was revised and extended, and the remaining Norse stories added. The English translation of Asbjørnsen and Moe is, in itself, an excellent and noted book. In 1871 an augmented edition of *Norse Folk Tales* was published under the names of the lifelong friends and collectors.

Norway is a small country with only about two and a half million inhabitants, but she has always given a good account of herself in literature. To Asbjørnsen and Moe's popular stories Jacob Grimm gave the palm for freshness and sincerity.

Notes on Folk Tales

In its widest sense, as a generic term for community composition, folk tale includes stories of at least five types: Myth, legend, fairy tale, nursery saga, and fable whenever the story is traditional and very old. Most fables are sophisticated and plainly bespeak individual authorship, as likewise do some myths and some fairy tales. In a more limited sense, when used as a specific term, as it is used in the indexes to these Readers, folk tale includes only the more domesticated myths and stories with myth elements, like *The Little Sister of the Sun* and *Why the Sea Is Salt*; and the simpler and more homely legends in the form of nursery sagas like *Boots and His Brothers*; and the traditional fairy tales, like *The Elves and the Shoemaker*. This is the sense in which the term "household tale," or "nursery tale," is usually understood. *The Queen Bee* is a nursery saga. For literary reasons the following distinction is sometimes made between fairy tale and nursery saga, which may both be household tales; in the fairy tale, the fairy or supernatural creature like a fairy is the chief actor; whereas in the nursery saga, the human being is the chief actor, is the hero. For this distinction the word "saga" is borrowed from the Norse language, where it signifies "hero-legend." The addition of the adjective "nursery" makes the phrase mean that the story is told of a child's hero or heroine. Often the hero is the youngest of three brothers and is supposed to be a ne'er-do-well: often the heroine is a neglected step-daughter or orphan.

Here are the formal definitions of these two types, set over against each other:

(1) **A Fairy Tale** is a narrative of imaginative events wherein the chief actors are beings other than man and the gods—beings who have the power utterly to destroy him. It is to be noted that the interest centers about the supernatural creature.

(2) **A Nursery Saga** is a narrative of imaginative events wherein is celebrated a human hero of more or less humble origin, a child's hero or heroine, who by native wit and energy (or supposed lack of wit and energy) together with the possession of a charm or secret helper is enabled to do

79

stupendous deeds, which bring material happiness. It is to be noted that the interest centers about the human hero, the boy or girl, not the fairy who may help or the charm that may win.

(3) **Drolls.** Comical folk tales are called drolls. Now, a nursery saga, we have just said, has a human hero; but a droll may have only a humanized hero. That is, the chief actor in a droll may be a cat or a mouse, a donkey or a pig, a gingerbread boy or a pancake; but as an actor it must seem human. In that fact resides the fun. A droll does not need to be satiric, though it generally is, but it must be jolly. The student will note the difference between a droll and a fable, though a fable also is satiric and has humanized animals and talking inanimate objects for actors. The forms are different. The fable is usually short and the nursery droll longer—the droll having the air of a saga. Besides, the fable is always in earnest; it is didactic and utilitarian, while the droll may be nothing but a laugh in narrative form. The idea of seriousness is the dividing line, too, between the nursery saga proper and the nursery saga droll. Someone has pleasantly conjectured that the usual nursery sagas must have been related originally by the women of the tribe, and the drolls by the men. The speaker had in mind, no doubt, such drolls as Hans in Luck and Thumbling. It is to be noticed that these stories retain the human hero, but are manifestly satiric, though they do not cease to be genial, especially Hans does not. The conjecture itself is droll and rather pat. It could hardly be proved, however.

THE FOLK TALES OF *THE PRIMER*

There are possibly two stories in *The Primer* not drolls, the first and the last. Since drolls are manufactured out of anything, however, tradition or not, we might call *The Little Red Hen* a pedagogical droll. In it, surely a lesson of cheerful industry is taught along with accurate ideas of planting and harvesting, grinding and baking. Or to be very modern, we might call it a domestic science droll, since the ideas of food sources and bread-making are prominent. The recollection that most of us have of the *The Little Red Hen*, I dare say, is the poetized version:

"'Oh, I will then,'

Said the little red hen,"

and so forth.

The Gingerbread Boy is a delightful hero, as is also the Pancake fellow. The children will not miss the expressions of countenance of these two as shown in the pictures and they should not miss the expressions of the other actors. The touches on the Gingerbread Boy are the most subtle, and should in themselves afford some pleasant oral composition on the part of the children. Since both these stories are tragedies that are not tragedies, the idea of what a droll is from a literary point of view might possibly be grasped by the more advanced pupils if not by all. They might be asked to make up drolls of their own. When we remember that Macaulay was reading the newspaper when he was four years old, that John Stuart Mill was studying Latin and Greek and had read all the high school classics in those subjects as well as in mathematics when he was eight, and that Robert Louis Stevenson had dictated a history of Moses before he could write, we need not hesitate to talk a bit rationally to our young subjects in the classroom. Some of them may be aching with genius and be ready to grow wonderfully if they only have the chance. Humor is a good pedagogue as well as a good civilizer. We cannot have too much of the right sort in school.

The Old Woman and the Pig might be considered the standard of the repetition droll. It is a typical folk tale also, insomuch as it reflects the simple attitude of early people toward the rest of creation. There was not for primitive man, as there is not for children today, any conscious barrier between the inanimate and the animate or the mere animal and the human. To the naïve mind the accident of never having heard a dog converse or a stick reply would not preclude the belief that upon occasions either could do so. Water and fire, oxen and ropes— why should they not talk as well as the butcher? and have their own affairs and their own prejudices? As for the sixpence, it is English, of whatever nationality the pig may be! The cumulative repetition idea must be very old, but this particular sequence could not go farther back in date than the first year of stiles, of rope manufacture, and of the differentiation of butchers. The sixpence is merely representative, one would suppose. If not, wise critics in dim future ages will be able to say definitely, considering that one point alone in connection with contemporaneous evidence, that the story did not originate in the years 1912, 1913, 1914, among any of the civilized tribes. Unless, perhaps, the whole composition were launched in 1914 as a droll on the coercive measures at that time in vogue.

The Boy and the Goat is a crybaby droll, on the same pattern. The illustrations are charmingly conceived. One is not quite sure, however, whether the disproportionate size of the bee is art or satire. The position of hero should justify the emphasis.

Chicken Little—or Chuck Luck, as he is sometimes called—is a brave youngster of much wisdom. He has his prototype in the world today, and has had it ever since man was man. The testimony of an eyewitness goes very far with most persons; few stop to consider whether or not snap judgment has accompanied the seeing and the hearing. However, Foxy Loxy is met sooner or later, and all is over for awhile, until another company with a Chicken Little for leader comes along. This story has many versions. The Norse, in Dasent's translation, is called *The Cock and the Hen that went to Dovrefell*. Here the hen finally outwits the fox, but only after he has devoured her followers.

Three Billy Goats Gruff is the other side of the shield. In this story the humanized heroes come off victorious without mistake. This is indisputably one of the best drolls in the world. It has virility with charm, the fairy tale quality with

naturalness, and the essentially oral style with naïve humor.
The mimetic element alone would make the story immortal. No
one who knows it can hear a goat go over a bridge and not think
of the line. The beat of the little hoofs is unmistakable. The
repetition of it is fascinating and the jollity and sprightliness
are irresistible. The fact that the sprightliness is enforced makes
the humor the better, as does also the fine brotherly love of the
Gruffs. They are united against a foe—they are united as many
a set of brothers is in the strength of the greatest. Daring and
cunning may avail if one only have substantial reference. The
two smaller Gruffs felt that they had it.

The troll belongs of right in a Norse tale. He is made to tease
Norse heroes and to be outwitted by them. He is usually a fiercer
creature than is here represented, however. In the original story
he has eyes as big as saucers and a nose as long as a poker. The
nose is characteristic of trolls. No wonder that the goat flew at
him, poked his eyes out, crushed him to bits, body and bone, and
tossed him into the water!

Little Tuppens, the next hero, might be Chicken Little's
less educated cousin. He has the family traits. The story as
here given is more interesting as a mere story and more logical
than either the German version, called in Grimm's collection
The Death of the Little Red Hen, or the Norse version called
The Cock and the Hen a-Nutting. The logic of the sequence,
however, makes one suspect the hand of the pedagogue. The
dwarfs, though a late addition by the kaleidoscopic process, are
not inappropriate. They belong to folk stories thoroughly and
may well join the sequence. This is a better version for school
children than Grimm's, both because of the information entailed
and because of the happy conclusion, though children love
funerals and buy hens and pet canaries with aesthetic pleasure.
The Norse tale just mentioned has a happy ending also, though
not the dwarf ending, as one would suspect. The kaleidoscope
has been shaken a number of times in this story. There are
many versions. The unnatural natural suspense is the charming
droll element retained in all.

Little Spider's First Web. Every teacher will recall with
what delight as a child he used to come upon a spider's web. The

exquisite workmanship never failed to hold his attention. The
last selection in *The Primer* gives opportunity for nature study,
not only of the spider but also of the bee, the ant, the cricket, the
butterfly, and the bird. The music of the outdoor world should
come under discussion also, and the question of how the insects
make their songs. The teacher should explain to city children
especially that the relative size of a bee and a cricket and of an
ant and a cricket is not always that given in the illustration.
Distinction should be made, too, between the cricket and the
grasshopper. General relative sizes are better expressed in the
last picture. The study of color, in which children revel, should
not be overlooked. *The Primer* is of necessity restricted, but
nature is not.

The connotation of the last line is excellent. This little
primer surely should make the children who read it very happy.
The drolls have in them the merriment of the ages; and through
the quaint structure of these narratives, repetition of words (a
necessity in a first book, but usually secured through a joy-
killing device) here turns out to be a delight, psychologically
attendant upon the art of real literature.

The Folk Tales of *First Reader*

First Reader contains five more drolls: the two English *The
Three Little Pigs* and *The Cat and the Mouse*; the German *The
Bremen Band*; the Russian *The Straw Ox;* and the Norse *The
Sheep and the Pig*.

The Three Little Pigs has the ancient well-honored *motif*
of the weak and supposedly stupid domestic animal's finally
overreaching the cunning of its wild enemies. That pleasing
thought is presented through the still more pleasing device of
repetition with jingle.

The Cat and the Mouse is similar, only it is not nearly so
spirited; besides, though it has the rhyme, it lacks the tripping
rhythm. The sequence idea is chief here.

The Bremen Band does not lack the rollicking effect of
a droll, and the gentle satire is evident, especially when one

remembers that this is a German production. The dramatic form is here good, and would be justified historically by other drolls in dramatic garb in Grimm's collection, like *Clever Hans,* if it were not justified in the first place by the native love of children for dramatic presentation.

The Straw Ox is quite as good in the droll way as *The Bremen Band,* and could easily be dramatized extemporaneously by the children. The story recalls the Tar Baby of the Uncle Remus narratives. The idea is as old as tar or older, and belongs to no one country. The Russian atmosphere of this tale is worthy of note. The bear is not an infrequent visitor at the doors of the scattered peasant huts of that vast land, as he is a not unfamiliar caller, likewise, on the few inhabitants of our own Yosemite valley. The other animals of the forest and wood seem hardly less familiar in a Russian door-yard than a bear. Russia is covered with thousands and thousands of square miles of beautiful forests that harbor all kinds of animals. Though there is the natural and primeval attitude of one creature's paw or fang against the other, there is a degree of brotherliness between man and beast not found in thickly populated communities from which wild animals have been altogether banished. In a primitive community, as here in the story, upon any occasion of mutual advantage all goes well. The old man's occupation of sharpening his knife as he sits by the cellar door is characteristic—though not only of Russian farmers, it must be admitted. But the dialogue that follows certainly suggests the proverbial source of the Muscovite peasants' winter garments, and when for these are substituted the other household necessities—honey, sheep, geese, and turnips—anyone who has been in Russia feels immediately at home.

The Sheep and the Pig is a fable-like droll. The fable element lies in the proverbs. The whole tale might be considered a pleasant fling at homely and conventional sayings. Even a child would smile at the rabbit's complacency when he says, "Good tools make good work." The next proverb is unquestionably droll also, both in statement and connotation. The pig's addition later is appropriate, too, coming from him. The repeated salutation and the summary of the story are in themselves worthwhile, as is indeed the whole composition. It has the unmistakable sturdy tang of Norse folk morality in it.

Wee Robin's Christmas Song has a Scottish tone corresponding with its source, and Wee Robin has Scottish sagacity. The story is a late production, obviously after the advent of Christianity in England. Animal epics, to which this story is allied by suggestion if nothing more, are a natural form growing out of the earlier community living of beasts and men. The story can hardly be called a droll. Wee Robin is too direct for a droll hero, and too aristocratic. The little pig was shrewd, but he won his way through plebeian methods. Wee Robin is intellectual and dignified. The greatest animal epic, or beast epic, is that of Reynard the Fox, but many of Reynard's adventures are droll; besides, he is generally a rascal. Like Wee Robin, he is sagacity itself. However, the sly fox in this narrative is only one of Reynard's less capable descendants. The whole tone of the version is late, even very modern. The appropriateness of the gift to Robin of Jenny Wren comes from the fact that the robins and the wrens feed together.

Little Two Eyes is one of the beautiful German nursery sagas of the Cinderella tradition. The ancient and primitive elements have been softened in both stories as given in our readers. The common properties are therefore not so apparent as they are in the German versions. The distinguishing incidents, rather, are retained, as they should be according to the law of good story transmission. The conception of persons with a varying number of eyes is ancient. Polyphemus, the chief of a race of one-eyed giants living in Sicily, had his one eye put out by Ulysses. Odin, the Norse god, is one-eyed. Jupiter, according to a Greek myth referred to by Grimm, has three eyes. The idea of a magic plant's springing from a buried portion of a killed or murdered creature is a common incident of folk tales. Teachers need not be afraid of these wild elements. Normal children are not shocked by them, because children themselves are in the folk tale stage of mental development.

Little Half Chick is also a late composition, with an artificial myth element in the attempt to account for the weathervane. The story is made up of ancient motifs, however, and is not uninterestingly told. The talking of Little Half Chick with the brook, the wind, and the fire is a true folk element. The idea of revenge is, of course, not exclusively Spanish, though at home, surely, in a Spanish tale. Naked justice is folk wisdom, and children appreciate it more than they do sentimentalism.

Little Topknot has both a fable element in the implied moral and the satire, and a myth element in the explanation of the absence of the large topknot on the hen. Such stories are called animal-myths, or *Pourquoi* stories. They answer the question why. There are many to be found in collections. "Popular Tales from the Norse" has one called *Why the Bear is Stump-tailed* and another, *The Cock, the Cuckoo, and the Black Cock* explaining the cries of the birds. Grimm's collection contains a similar story about the Bittern and the Hoopoe, and one about the Willow-Wren, and still another about the Sole, explaining why its mouth is on one side. Another called *The Fox and the Geese* is an animal-myth droll. A charming folk-myth like these, save that it is not about animals, is Grimm's *The Straw, the Coal, and the Bean*. The story accounts for the black seam on the bean.

The Fisherman and His Wife is a very old story and is widely diffused. Grimm mentions a number of variants, and reminds us that the feature of the wife's inciting her husband to seek high dignities is ancient in itself and dates from Eve. The greatest example in all literature is that of Lady Macbeth. It is the tragedy of human daring coupled with weakness that holds the reader and makes him return to a contemplation of such a course of events, even in its simplest form as a folk tale. High deeds ending disastrously have always been a tragic theme. In the Pomeranian version of this narrative the ominousness of the streak of blood on the water is in its way as fine a touch at the beginning as the short introductory scene of the witches is in *Macbeth*. The concomitant changing of the ocean with the increasing gravity of the events continues the effect. The impiousness of the fishwife's final ambition links her with Marlowe's Faustus as well as with Lady Macbeth. This criticism cannot be said to be artificial and forced, nor is it high-flown; for if the story be admitted to be true literature, as it indisputably is, then it must be admitted to be germane with all other true literature on the same theme. Moreover, indeed, Marlowe took his Faustus from popular legend. The Fisherman's story remained popular in form and is a nursery saga with childlike tone, but even the youngest reader or listener senses the philosophy.

The Lad and the North Wind has an entirely different atmosphere about it, but is equally good. It (a very happy story) is to the Fisherman (a very serious story) as *As You Like It* (a comedy) is to *Macbeth* (a tragedy), One must not be understood to say that *The Lad and the North Wind* is a droll. It is no more a droll than *As You Like It* is a farce. The Lad is a true nursery saga hero, the son of a poor woman. He has the sturdy confidence of his class. He does not hesitate to seek out the North Wind in its very abiding-place and demand justice. The good-humored action of the North Wind makes the reader feel the presence of destiny in the boy's life, and makes the critic suspect lingering myth elements in the narrative. The personification of the north wind is myth-like. "The tablecloth, the ram, and the stick," says Dr. Dasent, "are of the things of Wish, or Choice, about which the old mythology has so much to tell." Wish or Choice is Odin under another name, and its bounty is like the bounty of Odin. The Aryan school would naturally find much significance in the ram's money.

Whatever the hidden myth elements may be, this is a true nursery saga in its present form, as is attested by the fact of the boy hero's winning success from his opponents in repeated similar situations, first by initial bravery and second by a charm that he has secured through his persistence and good humor. The skeptical attitude of his mother, as well as the rascally behavior of the landlord, is also typical.

MOTHER GOOSE

Mother Goose rhymes belong to folklore, however recent they may seem to us. They are not antique, but they are old. Most of them have existed already two hundred years. A collection was published in Boston in 1719, and one in London in 1760. The author, or compiler, was a Boston woman who called herself "Mother Goose," taking the name then current in England and France for a teller of children's stories. (See Charles Perrault.) The rhymes have evidently undergone the folk literature process. They are today true English-American folk nursery material. Though they vary slightly at each oral recitation, yet they remain essentially always the same.

As the rhymes are a part of every American child's thinking, so are they likewise of the very folds and convolutions of American grown-up brains. For little foreign-born children attending the public schools and for the children of foreign-born parents nothing could be better as an instrument of Americanization. Our great problem is not so much to teach our language to immigrants—though that is part of our problem— as to lead our immigrants to think American-wise. Out of such bits as these rhymes, which are truly national, is made that large, good-humored, bold, yet conservative, practical, yet high-minded, scintillating, to some persons mystifying, to all persons (just at present, at least) vastly consequential and important thing, American thought.

In other words, one cannot *suddenly* think as a real American. One must have time to develop. Mere change of place does not give the power. From this fact come our anarchists, in and about New York; few if any of them are real Americans. The rougher sort are recent comers to our shores, and are drunk on the strong raw concoction of unexpected American license and old world politics. These unfortunates know nothing of the mental food of the nation as a whole. It is the true American food, however—the milk of kindliness and liberty, spiced with native humor—that indigenous Americans have grown up on. Indeed, such food is the nation's only hope of future existence. When the greater number of persons in this country cease to think as Americans, then there will be no America; for America, after all, is really not a place, but a state of mind.

And here at last is the wherefore of this digression. Since

a state of mind is made up of previous states of mind, if we care that a national state of mind should be perpetuated we, as educators, must see to it that the essential antecedents of that state of mind are perpetuated. Now, literature and deliberate teaching are the best means we have for a continuation of the best part of the past—its spirit.

The saving grace of humor. All this patriotic talk may for the moment seem far away from any connection with Mother Goose. Not so. Here is the relationship: One who has *not* been brought up on *Mother Goose* can hardly understand the Declaration of Independence; surely such a person cannot understand the humor of that document, which was meant above everything else to be practically true, not philosophically or literally true. Anyone who has been brought up on *Mother Goose* can understand it. He does not take things too literally— his own importance, for instance. It is the appreciation of the sense-of-nonsense and of the non-sense-of-pompous-sense that has made and preserved us as a nation. *Mother Goose* induces an appreciation of both. The greatest tyranny that has threatened modern times has grown up because the leaders of the countries primarily expressing it could not smile at themselves. An American's sense of humor saves him and makes him wise, because it always includes himself. Perhaps Americans are sane and tolerant insofar as they have been brought up on such searching rhymes as *Simple Simon* and *If All the World were Apple Pie*. It undoubtedly would have been a blessing to Europe, if Uncle Sam as a pedagogue, before the present war began, could have marched the chief militarists into the primary school and held them there until they learned by rote, with full appreciation, the last two stanzas of Simple Simon:

> Simple Simon went a-fishing,
> > For to catch a whale;
> All the water that he had
> > Was in his mother's pail.
>
> He went to catch a dicky-bird,
> > And thought he could not fail,
> Because he'd got a little salt
> > To put upon its tail.

OTHER SOURCES OF THE STORIES AND POEMS

CHRISTINA GEORGINA ROSSETTI (1830-1894)

Christina Rossetti wrote her first verses when she was twelve years old. They were addressed to her mother, on her mother's birthday, April 27, 1842, and were set up by Christina's grandfather Gaetano Polidori, on his private press. The Rossettis were a cultivated and interesting family.

Ten years a teacher. Christina's father, Gabriel Rossetti, was an Italian patriot and poet of ardent disposition and high character, who had come to England as a refugee in 1824. By the time Christina was born, December 5, 1830, he was established in London as a teacher of Italian, and within the year (1831), was appointed professor at King's College. He became well-known later as an Italian poet of much ability, and an expounder of what seemed to him to be the esoteric anti-papal significance of the Divine Comedy. He died when Christina was somewhat over twenty-three. For ten years before his death, he was an invalid, and Christina, with her sister Maria Francesca, three years her elder, helped her mother keep a day school for small pupils, first at Camden Town, then at Frome.

The mother. Christina's mother, it is said, was a remarkable woman, of great simplicity of nature and an unusual amount of common sense—self-controlled, just and kind, abhorring gossip and indolence. She was well-read and a lover of books, but most of all of life and accomplishments. She had no little business ability, always making both ends meet. She needed these virtues to get along more than passably well (as it seems she did) with her surprising and intellectual husband and progeny.

An unusual family. Christina's elder brother was Dante Gabriel Rossetti (1828-1882), the pre-Raphaelite painter and poet of great genius and exceedingly erratic temperament, who had, as might be expected, an unusual career. Once, long after her daughter Christina was famous and her husband's and her son's names were household names in England, Mrs. Rossetti said, "I always had a passion for intellect, and my wish was

91

that my husband should be distinguished for intellect, and my children, too. I have had my wish. I now wish that there was a little less intellect in the family, so as to allow for a little more common sense." In reading Christina's biography, one cannot but echo her mother's wish.

Best work early. Christina had a rare poetic gift of captivating quality, but she never improved. Her first work of any pretension is by far her best, *Goblin Market and Other Poems*, published in Cambridge and London in 1862 with designs by her brother Dante Gabriel. In this volume she attained a height she never afterwards reached, critics have agreed, though she published much. *Goblin Market* is a strange rich poem, with a haunting promise in it of future supreme greatness on the part of the author, a promise not fulfilled. Miss Rossetti did not discipline her own talent. She wrote too much, revised too little, and destroyed not enough.

Failed to improve. Like her brother, she seemed to have been impatient over her own compositions—to have wished simply to express herself and have done. She entertained no idea of polish and perfect completeness. Part of her charm no doubt comes from her very incompleteness; for it must be admitted that there is about her nonreligious verse, besides a sense of first writing, an air of the early morning dash of genius that might have disappeared with a careful noon-day revision. And surely we would not have her *Sing Song Nursery Rhymes* one whit labored! No, we would not; and yet, it cannot be denied that a considerate touch here and there from the same hand that made them would have improved even then. Christina Rossetti had as poor an ear for rhyme as had Mrs. Browning; and yet Mrs. Browning, as Dr. Garnett has pointed out, improved to the end of her days and Christina Rossetti never. Miss Rossetti's lapses are accordingly the more exasperating, since she disdained to notice them.

Christina was, like her sister Maria, profoundly religious, and gave the larger part of her time to church work and to writing pious compositions like *Seek and Find* (1879), *Called to be Saints* (1881), *Time Flies, a Reading Diary* (1885), *The Face of the Deep* (1892), *Verses* (1893). She wrote all these after her estrangement from her lover and suitor because of her high Anglican tendencies.

Her earlier work remains the better and more worldly
human, the more understandable, though everything she wrote
but *Goblin Market*, declares Richard Garnett, has a "taint."
Of peculiarity, one would think he meant, though he does not
explain. Before her distinctly religious period, she published her
stories called *Commonplace* (1870), her nursery rhymes called
Sing Song (1872), her tales for children, *Speaking Likenesses*
(1874).

Originality. Peculiarity, perhaps, along with originality
is Christina Rossetti's distinguishing mark. The very lilt of
her rhythm is original. This fact can be realized immediately
even by one who reads only her nursery rhymes. It might
almost be said that Christina Georgina Rossetti was the most
original writer that ever lived, surely the most original woman
writer. [Her *Dream Love, An End, L.E.L., A Birthday, An Apple
Gathering*, have been pronounced perfect lyrics, and she wrote
also good sonnets; but it is *Goblin Market* that gives her her
rank.]

Goblin Market is a narrative, in verse, based on the fancy
that goblins hold a market of rare fruits just at twilight and
sell only to young and beautiful maidens who will pay them
with a kiss or a curl, and at the same time stop and partake
with the sellers of the delicious dainties. These dainties have a
flavor beyond anything known to mortal palates except upon the
occasion of enchantment. Once tasted, the fruit creates what the
goblins intend shall be an unquenchable desire for more, which
they will never satisfy. Two sisters come across the meadow
at twilight; one lingers, is caught, buys, tastes, and shares in
the delirious revel. She is abandoned finally; and though she
comes again and again and lingers in the meadow to purchase
of the goblins, she never sees them. She hears only taunts and
insults. Her wild and feverish longing turns to despair, which
undermines her health and reason. Her sister saves her at last
by a great sacrifice, wherein the sister meets the goblins and
outwits them, though she is buffeted and tumbled unmercifully
by them before she escapes.

Allegory hangs all about this piece, and a rare descriptive
power permeates every line; but it is the music and rhythm
of the verse that astonishes, though it seems to result from

the luscious suggestiveness both physical and spiritual of the phraseology. The imagination that conceived *Goblin Market* was no common imagination.

SARA JOSEPHA HALE (1788-1879)

Mary Had a Little Lamb could be ranked as an American classic, if by "classic" were meant any piece of literature constantly used as a standard by way of reference and imitation, and universally familiar to the race that speaks the language of the piece. Like the rhymes of Mother Goose, this longer jingle is known by all true Americans. Every child should memorize it, not because of any intrinsic value, but because of the never-ending connotation.

Its author, Sarah Josepha Hale, knew children at first hand; for she had five of her own, left to her to support on the death of her husband when the eldest child was just seven years old (1822). David Hale had been an eminent lawyer and a well-read man; his widow, with some talent and a good deal of bravery, turned to writing for an income. In 1827 she published a novel, *Northwood*; in 1828 she became the editor of *The Ladies' Magazine* (Boston); and after nine years, when this publication was united with a Philadelphia monthly called *The Ladies' Book*, Mrs. Hale continued in the editorship. But before the consolidation she had published "Flora's Interpreter, or the American Book of Flowers and Sentiments" (Boston, 1832).

Combined plant study and literature. The title of this collection and that of the next lets us gently into the minds and hearts of American women a century ago. We hardly need to turn the leaves of the books to ascertain what is there. In the first, two hundred sixteen plants and flowers are described, with poetic interpretations accompanying them. By way of introduction the author says, "In arranging this little work it was my purpose to combine, with the names and remembrances of flowers, a selection of sentiments from our best poets. I hoped my experiment would give an increased interest to botanical researches among young people, at least, and among all classes would promote a better acquaintance with the beauties of our own literature."

Another experiment. This "experiment" is very quaint; but the next title and preface sound still more quaint, and charmingly timid, when we think of the bold claims of our modern asserters of woman's ability: "The Ladies' Wreath; a selection from the Female Poetic Writers of England and America, with original notices and notes: prepared especially for Young Ladies. A Gift-Book for All Seasons. By Mrs. Hale. Boston: 1837."

Her ideals. In her preface she says in part: "Two principles have guided my selections: one, to admit no poetry unless its aim was 'upward and onward'; the other, to allow place to those writers only whose style had some peculiar stamp of individuality, which marked their genius as original; and I have sought to give characteristic specimens from each.

"I am aware that there are critics, who always speak of the 'true feminine style,' as though there was only one manner in which ladies could properly write poetry ... The truth is, woman has not such unlimited range of subjects as man; but in the manner of treating those within her province, she has a freedom as perfect as his; and the delicate shades of genius are as varied and distinctly marked in the one sex as its bold outlines are in the other. There are more varieties of the rose than of the oak."

The last sentence is delicious. It is an epitome of the woman question in the first forty years of the nineteenth century. The index to Part I of *The Ladies' Wreath* presents among the English authors the name of Jane Taylor; and the index to Part II, among the American authors, that of Mrs. Hale herself. In view of her preface, it is truly delightful to see that she has allowed place to eleven of her own poems.

PHOEBE CARY (1824-1871)

Phoebe Cary is hardly ever mentioned without her sister Alice, since the two lived together all their lives and since their poems are now published together in a well-known edition. Alice was the elder and the more prolific writer, but both women are interesting for their example of independence and attainment in the days before the education of woman was much considered. Alice and Phoebe did not have a very pleasant childhood and early young womanhood. They discovered the truth of the old fairy tales about stepmothers who were not kind. Their stepmother was not kind. She did not refuse them food, to be sure, but what they considered more important—candles to read and write by in the evening. She was impatient with their desire to learn. She kept them busy with the household work during the day (and they were willing enough to help), but she refused to hear to candlelight improvement after the work was done. The girls used to resort to the device of a saucer with lard and a bit of rag, concealed during the day and brought out after the other members of the family had gone to bed. At the age of eighteen Alice was writing for the press, and continued to write more or less surreptitiously at home for ten years or more.

The sisters in New York. In 1852 the two sisters left their home, where they were born, near Cincinnati, and went to New York to make their living with their pens. Alice is said to have been an indefatigable writer, contributing to the *Atlantic Monthly*, *Harper's*, *Putnam's*, *The New York Ledger*, and *The Independent*. Phoebe wrote, too, though not so much. She took the larger share of the housework, since Alice was not strong in body as she. Phoebe was always the more buoyant of the two, and the more brilliant and witty in conversation.

The sisters became prominent in New York literary circles. Indeed, they had a circle quite of their own, also, that gathered around them on Sunday evenings, when they made a point of being "at home" to anyone who cared to talk books or other sense. The little assemblies were in no way fashionable, but in every way high-toned. Such men as Horace Greeley, Bayard Taylor, John Greenleaf Whittier, Thomas Bailey Aldrich, and Justin McCarthy were frequenters, and almost every person of any literary pretensions in New York found his way to their door sooner or later during the fifteen years that the sisters kept open house.

Alice and Phoebe Cary died within a few months of each other, Alice in New York, and Phoebe in Newport, where she had been taken in hope of recovery.

Phoebe Cary's publications were as follows: *Poems and*

Parodies (1854), *Poems of Faith, Hope, and Love* (1868), *Hymns for All Christians* (1869). (About one-third of the volume published by the Reverend Charles F. Deems was by Alice and Phoebe Cary.) Phoebe Cary is the author of the familiar hymn called "Nearer Home," beginning with the words, "One sweetly solemn thought." She wrote it when she was seventeen.

ALFRED TENNYSON (1809-1892)

For forty-two years Tennyson was poet-laureate of Great Britain, and his was the leading name in English letters. Whether he was the greatest poet writing in English in the nineteenth century used often to be discussed. The answer is largely a matter of taste. It is obvious that he is not so intense and vital as Browning, and not so quiet and deep as Wordsworth. The final judgment by many readers is somewhat like this: Of the three, Tennyson is the most uniform in excellence; his average is the highest, if one may speak mathematically. He wrote fewer unreadable lines, and his best conceptions are always high, though not so high as the best of Browning, perhaps, or the best of Wordsworth.

His eye and ear. Tennyson has more than anyone else, however, even more than Wordsworth, the seeing eye when he looks on nature; and he has conspicuously, more than Browning and more than other poets of the nineteenth century, the musical ear.

His first volume to create any general notice, *Poems by Alfred Tennyson*, 1832, astonished the public by just that quality of liquid rhythm which we now know to be truly Tennysonian. The volume included "The Lady of Shalott," "The Miller's Daughter," "The Palace of Art," "The Lotus Eaters," and "A Dream of Fair Women." However, the *Quarterly Review* fell on it with savage criticism, and Tennyson was silenced for ten years; but when he spoke again in 1842, he spoke with the same silver tongue. Tennyson worked hard and diligently, but it would seem that he himself thought his ear for meter a natural gift; for in speaking once of his childish poems, which were never published, he said that as he remembered them they were all perfect in meter. He began to write verse when he was eight. Before his thirteenth year he had composed an "epic" of 60,000 lines, and his father had predicted, "If Alfred should die, one of our greatest poets will have gone."

No doubt Tennyson's home schooling had much to do with his early appreciation of poetic form. It is recorded that he told Edmund Gosse once that the Reverend George Tennyson, his father and first schoolmaster, would not let him leave home for college until on successive days he had recited from memory the whole of the Odes of Horace. We know that it was the charming picturesqueness of Lincolnshire, his birthplace, that trained Tennyson's "seeing eye."

Basis of fame. The volume called *Enoch Arden* (1864), of which thousands of copies were sold at once, became the most popular of Tennyson's publications except *In Memoriam* (1850), and was translated into Danish, German, Latin, French, Dutch, Hungarian, and Bohemian. The *Idylls of the King* (1859) had already been received with great popular favor. These narratives are, in a way, the most considerable body of Tennyson's work. They form his "epic," if one may so speak, though they were written at various times and only more-or-less artificially united later. The fact that they are founded on a national legend will insure their continued favor over other poems. Alone they would perpetuate the chief Tennysonian qualities of style— ideal portraiture, picturesqueness, exquisite finish and melody, ornateness, moral elevation, and microscopic observation of nature. Tennyson rose only occasionally to real passion, and seldom, if ever, to vehemence. "Rispah" is truly intense, as is also much of the idyll of "Guinevere."

Observation of nature. It is to Tennyson's microscopic observation of nature that the attention of school children should be especially directed. They might be inspired by Tennyson when they could not be driven by the ordinary "nature study" to observe outdoor life closely. He challenges them with allusions. They might ask themselves, if ash buds *are* black in March, if willows *do* whiten, if little breezes dusk and shiver through a wave, if the river runs with an inner voice. Does a swallow seem to chase itself with its own wild will? Does a cloud cling all night to a hillside, and with the dawn, ascending, let the day strike where it clung?

Does swimming vapor slope across a glen, and, putting forth an arm, creep from pine to pine? Does a cedar spread dark-green *layers* of shade? Is there such a sight as yellow sails upon a yellow sea? Tennyson spent every summer from his childhood up by the ocean. Someone who doubted his accuracy on this last description of home scenery went once to observe, and came back a wiser, if discomfited, critic.

JANE TAYLOR (1783-1824)

Twinkle, Twinkle, Little Star is as much a classic as *Mary Had a Little Lamb*, and is as well-known in America, though *Twinkle, Twinkle* is British. The author, Jane Taylor, was born in Red Lion Street, London, of a literary family. Soon after Jane's birth, the family moved to the country, and in time became known to fame and to history as the Taylors of Ongar, in distinction from the Taylors of Norwich, who were also literary.

A family of writers. The father, the mother, the brother, the sister, and Jane herself, the youngest daughter of the Taylors of Ongar, all wrote, all became prominent as contributors to magazines for young people, and as authors of books for children and of instructive composition in general. It is said that the literary productiveness of Isaac Taylor of Ongar, his collaterals and their descendants led Sir Francis Galton in his inquiry into the laws and consequences of heredity and genius (1869), to illustrate from the history of this family his theory of the distribution through heredity of intellectual capacity.

The home a college. It may be that the great anthropologist forgot the importance of environment, but it is evident that environment counted for much in the accomplishment of this family. First the father, an expert engraver and at the same time a nonconformist preacher, maintained at home a strict system of education for his children, watching over them in their work and play. Very little time was wasted. Books were read aloud at meals as in a monastery. Beautiful charts engraved by the father were used by the children in studying their history. They would insert names and dates and other small bits of information, and in turn

themselves learned engraving as well as history. The brother
learned also to paint, and later engraved designs for his father's
and sisters' books, and painted miniatures, an excellent one of
Jane, which is carefully preserved by the British government, as
are also beautiful examples of the father's work. His delicate set
of designs for Thomson's *Seasons*, for instance, can be found in
the display of engravings in the British Museum.

Poetry not encouraged. The children's play was as intense
and jolly as their work; but, strange to say, neither the father
nor the mother encouraged verse making. Jane and Ann used
to indulge in it on the side. They were always imagining stories
and drafting introductions and prefaces for books, sometimes
in verse. Jane's first practical use of her talent was in the form
of a request to her parents for a small garden for herself. She
presented her argument in "five well-tuned stanzas, in the metre
of *John Gilpin*." Jane's first printed poem was *The Beggar's Boy*,
appearing in 1804 in a small annual called *The Minor's Pocket
Book*, to which her sister had been correspondent for six years.

Beginning of children's literature. In 1804, also,
a number of Jane's poems appeared between the covers of
a book—that epoch-making little volume succinctly titled,
Original Poems for Infant Minds by Several Young Persons. The
several young persons were Jane, Ann, and their brother Isaac.
This book marked the beginning of the era of good literature
for children. The world immediately saw what had been
lacking, and recognized the suggestiveness and worth of this
contribution. The volume was almost immediately reprinted in
America, and was translated into German, Dutch, and Russian.
It ran through fifty editions in England alone before the century
was out.

Rhymes for the Nursery, by the Authors of "Original Poems,"
appeared in 1806, and *Hymns for Infant Minds* sometime
afterwards. The *Hymns* ran through one hundred editions in
England, and is, perhaps, all in all, the best contribution of
the little firm of authors. Jane's hymns are said to be less good
as literature than her sister's, though they are all simple and
direct. It is a question how appropriate the term "literature" is
for any instructive or pedagogical writing, however popular and
however enduring; but perhaps with the qualifying phrase "for

children" the work of these sisters may be called real literature.

The year Ann began to write for the *Minor's Pocket Book* was the year of the *Lyrical Ballads* by Wordsworth and Coleridge, which ushered into the larger field of English letters the age of simplicity in diction and thought. Part of the popularity of the songs for children by the Taylor sisters was consequent, therefore, no doubt, upon the larger movement and the preparation of the public mind for simple things. It is noteworthy that Ann's best verse in the 1804 volume is called *My Mother*; and Jane's, *The Cow and the Ass*. To those who know the *Lyrical Ballads* this choice of subject is revealing.

The best edition of Ann and Jane's verse may be found in libraries today under the title *Poetical Works* by Ann and Jane Taylor. It is one volume, containing the Original Poems, Rhymes, and Hymns. *Twinkle, Twinkle, Little Star* is tenth in this book.

During the last twelve years of her life, Jane lived with her brother at Ifracombe. After her death he wrote a beautiful and marvelously delicate memoir of her. Jane Taylor's portrait was displayed at the Chicago World's Fair in 1893 in the Gallery of Distinguished English Women.

Aesop (619?-564?)

Aesop is a legendary person. No one is quite sure when he lived. Tradition places him somewhere in the sixth century before Christ as a counselor at the court of Croesus, the Lydian king. He is supposed to have been a Greek slave and very ugly, and to have won his way to recognition by his wit in telling a story and applying the moral.

Stories written by another. Aesop wrote nothing, it is said, but his fame lived and his stories lived. The individual narratives circulated orally at first. Finally, in 1447 Planudes, a monk of Constantinople, put forth in prose a collection of about three hundred stories, which today bears the name Aesop. That collection is, no doubt, the source of the fables in our readers.

Stories widely scattered. These fables spread all over the ancient world. One is not surprised to find *The Boy and the Fox* and *The Town Mouse and the Country Mouse* called Norse tales; they are no doubt Norse Aesopian fables. They are told in every tongue. The Filipinos have an analogue about a jar of cooked rice that a boy kicked and upset just as he was dreaming of the fortune he should make out of it. The boy and the jar are Aesop's girl and the basket of eggs at home in the Pacific. *The Town Mouse and the Country Mouse* has always proved attractive to literary men. In the fifteenth century it was done into Chaucerian stanzas by Henryson in his book of Morall Fables of Esope the Phrygian, and was there called *The Uplondish Mous and the Berger Mous*. It was done again by Prior and Montague in the latter part of the seventeenth century and pointed in satire at Dryden.

The use of the fable. The fable as a type of narrative has always been used for satire. It is the prime didactic form, brief, neat, symbolic. Sometimes it has a maxim attached, and sometimes it has not; but the lesson is always clear and acute and always practical. There are three classes of fables: (1) the rational, in which the actors and speakers are solely human beings or the gods of mythology living as human beings; (2) the nonrational, in which the heroes are solely animals, vegetables, or inanimate objects; and (3) the mixed, in which men speak with animals or inanimate objects. The second class is called the Beast Fable and is perhaps the most popular.

It is a question whether the word "Aesop" did not originally signify just what our word "fable" signifies today—a type of narrative, not a man.

HANS CHRISTIAN ANDERSEN (1805-1875)

In Hans Christian Andersen the world has at last caught the folk-story author at his work. We can name him, and definitely locate him in place and time, and feel insofar very well satisfied. And yet there is something about this strange figure which we do not comprehend, just as there is something weird and fascinating about ancient folk stories which we shall never comprehend. We know that Andersen was born in the Danish city of Odense, April 2, 1805, of poor and shiftless parents; that he went up to Copenhagen to learn to be a dramatic writer

102

and failed; and that, holding a scholarship granted him by the king in order that he might prepare for the university, he showed himself neither brilliant nor docile; and that finally he became famous, visiting the great and the near-great and being visited by them in return; and witnessed one day when he had a frightful toothache and could not enjoy things very much, a literary jubilee in which he was honored as a writer of the first rank of one kind of composition; and saw later a monument erected to him in his lifetime, and died August 1, 1875, in quite a definite way and was followed to his grave by a magnificent state funeral procession. Yet, we say, though we know this history, there is something elusive and mysterious about Hans Christian Andersen.

Disliked the work he did. He fretted all his life because he could not write novels and dramas. He did children's stories and became noted for them against his will. He chafed under the fact, but kept writing out his graceful, juvenile fancies for thirty-seven years. He could not stop if he would, it seemed. Strange to say, also, he was not fond of children, nor they of him when they met him, though they always loved his charming letters. His appearance was anything but prepossessing: he was "limp, ungainly, awkward, odd, with long lean limbs, broad flat hands, and feet of striking size. His eyes were small and deep-set, his nose very large, his neck very long." By some trick of fate, some wicked decree of a malicious witch, he was destined to be always the loathly one of fairy tales, the prince in disguise. Perhaps he was, rather, the airy fancy of eternal childhood embodied for once and walking among us, but in ugly encasement, lest the Danes should wish to keep it forever for themselves, held a prisoner in their own small country.

A wanderer. Hans Christian Andersen, the boy, the young man, the mature adult, never had a home until he was sixty-one years old. He wandered all over Europe and the near East, writing travel sketches and attempting novels and dramas. The best of the travel books is *In Sweden* (1851), the best of the novels is *Only a Fiddler* (1837). This grown-up person took no part in the politics of the day and never seemed to understand other grown-up persons and their ways, though the spirit within longed as a child longs to be famous among them.

Hans Christian Andersen the *spirit* never grew up. It was always a child, a little bit spoiled, a little bit petulant, not comprehending its own genius, not knowing its own happiness, but sweet and good and lovable when expressing itself naturally. It lives and breathes and has a home forever in the *Picture Book Without Pictures* and the *Tales and Stories* for children.

Stories are childlike. They are not so much for children, these stories, as they are of children. They take liberties with the language as children do: they make mistakes in rhetoric and syntax as children do; they use the *ohs* and *ahs* of the nursery and substitute action and imitation for description; and, withal, have a teasing suggestion of rationality and worldly wisdom about them as children sometimes have. Above all, we say, they possess an air of eternality, a semblance of having come from far back in time and of going far forward, not indeed as children have—for children do not live forever—but as childhood has. The faults of the stories have many times been catalogues, but each assayer finally stops off with the general summary: "Perfect of their kind! No one else puts himself so wholly in the child's place and looks at nature so wholly with the child's eyes as Andersen." This consensus of opinion seems to establish our theory. It may be that Hans Christian Andersen was merely childhood writing itself down.

Mary Howitt's translation of Andersen's stories introduced them into England (1843-1846). A later translation was made by Somers (1893).

The Fir Tree and *Little Maia*, modern "fairy tales," are not Hans Christian Andersen at his best, but *The Brave Tin Solder* is. That little story has become a classic, loved by grown folk, perhaps, more than by children. It reveals all of Andersen's qualities. For absorbing interest, children would doubtless choose *The Tinder Box* or *Big Claus and Little Claus*; but the bits of philosophy uttered by the Tin Soldier and implied throughout his story draw the mature reader back and back again to a contemplation of the artless art of the narrative.

ROBERT LOUIS STEVENSON (1850-1894)

Robert Louis Stevenson seems to people of this country very companionable and brotherly, very much American. He married an American and lived in the United States two or more years. For *Scribner's Magazine* he did some of his best work. It was an American publisher, Mr. S.S. McClure, who advanced the means enabling Stevenson to start his cruise in the Pacific and build his home Vailima near Apia, Samoa, in the South Seas.

His personality. Stevenson, however, was a Scotsman by birth and predilection. He came of a line of civil engineers and lighthouse builders, sturdy, moral folk, who served the world seriously and well. It was the moral fiber, inherited and cultivated, and the tough Scotch persistence of the lighthouse builders that made Robert Louis come through successfully so many hard fought battles with death, and enabled him to smile grimly at each weak triumph. Stevenson's continued plucky fight won him many friends. His fine cheerful spirit, his merry appreciation of life in general (which was so often hard and cruel with him), his devotion to his art against all hazards, and his romantic career brought him more fame than his literary productions brought him or will bring him, though his productions are all but of the first order if not of the first.

Versatility. What is implied in the last statement is that Stevenson was particularly a stylist, but no one lives by style alone. The charm of his personality is what makes this man immortal. It is constantly noted with wonder that his fame is disproportionate with the numerical circulation of his works. He "handled with distinction nearly all the known forms" of writing, but not one of his creations stands out so plainly in our minds as Stevenson himself stands. It is not only because Stevenson is near us in time that we know him. Most of us never saw him; he died a long time before we were born and is buried in a lofty grave overlooking the sea. The world remembers him because he expressed himself and his own peculiar way of thinking in all he wrote. Whether some of his essays are mannered, or not, is beside the point. They are surely his essays and not another man's, and successive sets of reader will continue to enjoy them—especially will young readers, trained to an appreciation of niceties of diction. Part of Stevenson's mission was to induce the modern public to like delicacies.

His best writings. He wrote with a naked, bold hand sometimes, and affected the unstudied romance like *Treasure Island*, which brought him his first popularity (1882); and *Kidnapped*, a semi-historical murder case; and the sensational delineation of a dual personality, *Dr. Jekyll and Mr. Hyde*, which was published as a "shilling shocker" (1886) and succeeded. But after all, in spite of his instant popularity in it and his standing as a leader calling young writers back to romance, Stevenson is primarily an analyst and a discriminating weigher of motives. Two of the strongest tales in Scottish literature are his *Thrawn Janet* and *The Merry Men*, one "a study of satanic possession," and the other of "conscience and imagination haunted to the overthrow of reason by the terrors of the sea." *Markheim*, done for *Unwin's Christmas Annal* in America, is another such study. *The Master of Ballantrac*, the scenes of which are partly laid in the country around Saranac Lake in the Adirondacks, where the Stevensons spent the winter of 1887-1888, is at once also one of the writer's best tales and one of his most vivid and searching delineations of mental states. No; Stevenson was no loose-jointed, cheap romancer, but always the artist, and especially the artist in words. One is impressed by his phrases more than by the whole piece.

His aptness of phrase and his quaint fancy are the charm of *A Child's Garden of Verse*. Though his rhymes are meager and often repeated, they are exquisite and delightful at their best, and the poet's attitude is impeccably naïve and sweet. Critics have said that in all his varied composition Stevenson invented no new form of literary expression, unless the verses of *A Child's Garden* may be so considered.

These verses were begun in 1883 in the chalet "La Solitude," a little house in France, where the writer, for the first time in his life, passed a respite of nearly a year from acute illness. They were finished in 1885 at "Skerryvore," the house bought and given him by his father in hope that the author could continue to live in the land of his birth; but he could not. Hemorrhages and prostration occasioned by the climate drove him out. Stevenson called his Scotch home "Skerryvore" after the famous lighthouse designed by his Uncle Alan.

The search for health. Robert Louis Stevenson's search for health is well known. It was remarkable for the sick man's jaunty courage and his unremitting labor meanwhile. He never complained. After his father's death in 1887, he sailed with his mother (Magaret Isabella Balfour), wife (Fanny Osbourne), and stepson (Lloyd) for New York. He spent the winter at Saranac, and began his cruise of the Pacific, June 26, 1888, in the schooner-yacht *Casco* (Captain Otis). He touched at various ports and remained six months at Honolulu, from January to June, 1889. From there he set off in a rough trading vessel, the *Equator*, and found himself in the harbor of Apia, Samoa, at Christmas time. He liked the climate so well that he purchased four hundred acres on the mountain side, had a clearing made, and his frame house erected, which later received an addition. He called his home "Vailima," or Five Rivers. He brought out his mother, whom he had left at Honolulu, and settled down in comparative health and great peace and happiness with his wife, his mother, his stepson, and later his stepdaughter (Isobel), who acted as an amanuensis.

The new lord was kind to the natives, and became very popular among them. They considered him a chief, and came to him for advice. He served them with devotion and political wisdom, redressing their wrongs. He gathered his immediate retainers about him daily for family prayers. Some of the beautiful things he said for them are published in the tiny volume called *Prayers Written for Family Use at Vailima*, edited by Mrs. Stevenson after her husband's death.

Stevenson worked early and late at Vailima, for he was never finally freed, as Tennyson was, from the gnawing anxiety of money-getting. In January, 1893, he had a stroke of illness accompanied with bronchitis, and was both unable and forbidden to talk. He carried his work gaily on, however, dictating in the deaf-and-dumb alphabet the story he had been writing. The next December he died. Death came quite unexpectedly with the rupture of a blood-vessel in the brain; but he went as he would have wished, gaily, conversing with his wife. He had been working hard all the morning on his half-finished book, *Hermiston*, which he judged the best he had ever written, and had come to her, as he always came, for criticism and confirmation. He had received it; and they were celebrating Stevenson's consciousness of his full powers, when he was taken suddenly, falling on his knees at her feet. He was buried the next day on a narrow shelf of rock on the summit of Mount Vaea, whither he was carried by his devoted native friends, forty of them cutting a path up the steep face of the mountain, and twenty others of the more immediate household preceding to dig the grave or following bearing the coffin shoulder-high up the rugged way. Nineteen Europeans and sixty Samoans climbed the height. All night long before, the Samoans had watched at his side, kneeling and kissing his hand each in turn before taking up the watch, and all the morning they and their relatives and friends had brought flowers and rare mats as offerings to the chief whom they loved, their Tusitala, teller of tales.

Stevenson wrote his own Requiem. One need say nothing of how fine it is: the brave man speaks for himself:

> Under the wide and starry sky,
> Dig the grave and let me lie.
> Glad did I live and gladly die,
>   And I laid me down with a will.
>
> This be the verse you grave for me:
> Here he lies where he longed to be;
> Home is the sailor, home from sea,
>   And the hunter home from the hill.

SIR JAMES MATTHEW BARRIE (1860-1937)

Barrie, "that modest little man," as everyone is prompted to call him behind his back, whatever may be the correct appellation to his face, was born in Scotland, the realm that has given us more than one lovable author—"Bobbie Burns," "Sir Walter," "R.L.S.," and, not least by any means, "Barrie." Sir James M. Barrie, the author of *A Window in Thrums* (1889), *The Little Minister* (1891), *Margaret Ogilvy* and *Sentimental Tommy* (1896), *Tommy and Grizel* (1900), *The Little White Bird* (1902), *Peter Pan in Kensington Gardens* (1906), *Peter and Wendy*

(1911), and other delectable compositions before and since.

Barrie has made more money by his pen than has any other single living author. He has taken the stage by storm, perhaps one would better say, by sweetness and light. His dramas are *The Professor's Love Story* (1895), *The Little Minister* (adapted—1897), *The Wedding Guest* (1900), *Quality Street, The Admirable Crichton, Little Mary* (1903), *Peter Pan* (1904), *Alice-sit-by-the-fire* (1905), *What Every Woman Knows* (1908), *The Legend of Leonora, The Mill, The Adored One* (1913).

Auld Licht Idylls, When a Man's Single, A Window in Thrums, The Little Minister, Sentimental Tommy, and *Margaret Ogilvey* are said to have autobiographical material in them. All good books have, of course. The quiet, delightful home living of a Scotch mother and her son is portrayed in *Margaret Ogilvey* .

Barrie wrote until his death in 1937. He had his schooling at Dumfries Academy and Edinburgh University.

ELIZA LEE CABOT FOLLEN (1787-1860)

Eliza Lee Cabot Follen is remembered as a writer of anti-slavery hymns and songs, as editor of *The Child's Friend*, and as the author of a volume of poems and of the memoirs (five volumes) of her husband, Dr. Follen. Dr. Follen was at one time professor of German literature at Harvard, and before that appointment had escaped to America as a refugee from Switzerland, whither he had fled from the government detectives of Russia, Austria, and Prussia, who wanted him (1824) for having disseminated revolutionary doctrines in their realms. Like his wife, Dr. Follen became, under the inspiration of William Ellery Channing, a zealous opponent of slavery and a Unitarian in faith. Dr. Follen lost his place at Harvard because of his outspoken views, and for the remainder of his life, a short time, devoted himself almost entirely to the anti-slavery movement. He died in an accident in 1831, leaving to Mrs. Follen the support and education of their son. Mrs. Follen proved equal to the task, preparing successfully her own son and a number of other pupils for Harvard.

Mrs. Follen wrote, besides the books already mentioned, *Well-spent Hour* (1827), *The Skeptic* (1835), *Twilight Stories* (1858), and *Home Dramas* (1859).

CHARLES KINGSLEY (1819-1875)

Charles Kingsley was born and bred an English country gentleman, but he was made a thorough aristocrat at heart by a brutal sight he witnessed when he was a boy of twelve. He was attending grammar school at Bristol, and from a window looked down on the besotted, unreasoning action of the mobs in the Bristol riots. Later he became a clergyman and a philanthropist of much renown, but he never forgot this unfortunate experience. He was a delicate, sensitive child at the time and very reserved—"proud," his schoolmates said. They did not like him, nor understand him. He was not fond of regular sports, as most English boys are, but preferred to make long excursions for plants or geological specimens. Later, when a member of Magdalene College, Cambridge, he was better liked, because better understood. Indeed, he became popular when he indulged in rowing and boxing. He still enjoyed long excursions into the country, but made them now as part of his course in equestrian lectures on geology. Kingsley was not a close student, though he won some honors in mathematics and the classics during the latter part of his college days.

Curate and professor of history. He took orders when he was twenty-three, and went as a country curate to a desolate, uncultivated, poor, illiterate, and unwholesome parish on the borders of Windsor forest. Here he married, here he established his home, here he finally died, after working very hard with true and profound sympathy for the poor. Kingsley did not live so long as he would have lived had he taken more vacations and devoted himself less assiduously to his "duties." He tried to teach the dumb-headed to read, the careless to think, the wicket to cease their stealing and be good, the wanderers to settle down and prosper, and many unsatisfied and restless characters to accept Christianity and be at peace. Yet Kingsley had his own doubts, and went through periods of much stress and anxiety.

110

For nine years (1860-1869) he was professor of modern history at Cambridge, going up from his parish for his lectures; but though he did the young men much good as an inspiring friend, he found the work unsatisfactory finally and his own temperament unsuited to the new spirit of precise scholarship abroad in the faculty. He withdrew to concentrate his efforts on his writing and his parish work.

Preaching and writing. In 1859 Kingsley was appointed chaplain to Queen Victoria, and later received a canonry at Chester, which was exchanged in 1873 for one at Westminster. As a preacher, Kingsley is said to have been vivid and earnest, speaking out as plainly to the nobility and fashionable folk as to the poor. He had the virtue also of being unsentimental and not mawkish when addressing the common people. *The Message of the Church to Working Men* is one of his great speeches, and his *Twenty-five Village Sermons*, preached early in his life at Eversley, are unsurpassed. Some of Kingsley's socialistic writings have not been published otherwise than as they appeared originally in *The Christian Socialist* and the journal called *Politics for the People*. Kingsley had a son, an engineer in America, whom he visited (1874). While here, he preached a series of sermons which were published (1875) under the title *Sermons Delivered in America*.

The novels, like everything else the author did, were done with a purpose. They appeared as follows: *Yeast* (1849), *Alton Locke* (1849), *Hypatia* (1859), *Westward Ho* (1855), *At Last* (1871). The children's books were also done with a purpose. The moral teacher is never absent: *The Heroes* (Greek Tales) (1856), *Water-Babies* (1863), *Madam How and Lady Why* (1869). Kingsley's poems came out at various times. They can be found in a two-volume edition (Macmillan, 1884).

The Lost Doll is a little song from the *Water-Babies*. It was sung by the fairy Do-as-you-would-be-done-by when she was cuddling Tom for the first time (chap. v). All the other babies were pleased with the ditty. The author does not say whether Tom liked it, but remarks, "What a silly song for a fairy to sing. And what silly water-babies to be quite delighted with it!" Hundreds of land-babies seem to enjoy it, as well.

JOHN KENDRICK BANGS (1862-1922)

John Kendrick Bangs was born "forty-five minutes from Broadway," or, in other words, at Yonkers, New York. One thinks of him as a city man and a humorist, though he did the commonwealth the very humdrum and substantial service of being president of the Halsted School, Yonkers, for ten years (1894-1904). He served on the editorial staff of the following periodicals: *Life, Drawer, Literary Notes, Harper's Magazine, Literature, Harper's Weekly, Metropolitan Magazine,* and *Puck.* His subjects reveal the humorist. He has written on "The Idiot," "The Idiot at Home," "The Inventions of the Idiot," "Mr. Munchausen," "Mrs. Raffles." "The Little Elf," though a verse selection, represents very well his light touch.

BJØRNSTJERNE MARTINIUS BJØRNSON
(1832-1910)

Brandes, the Danish critic, once said that to name the name of Bjørnstjerne Bjørnson is like hoisting the Norwegian flag. Brandes did not mean merely that the name is truly Norse, but that the personality and career it represents are also Norse. The flag connotation is good, for Bjørnson was an intellectual militant, fighting to win for his countrymen a national consciousness in a literature distinct and contributive. He worked through poetry, stories, the novel, the drama, oratory, and personal influence.

Until 1814, Norway belonged to Denmark, and until then the literary traditions of the two countries were one. With the separation began an intellectual stirring in the North, which was destined to show itself in force in the next generation. The opening of the first great era in Norwegian letters is marked by Bjørnson's *Synnøve Solbakken,* 1857, "a simple tale of peasant life, an idyl of the love of a boy and girl," but an intimate revelation of Norwegian character in a style at once realistic and individual.

His great work. Bjørnson became in the next fifteen years the spokesman of his race. During that time he wrote dramas founded on the Norse sagas. Sigurd Slembe, the best, has been termed by one of Bjørnson's admirers the noblest masterpiece of all modern literature. Bjørnson said that his style was founded on the sagas; and he gave as the fundamental principle of his literary method the endeavor "To see the peasant in the light of the sagas and the sagas in the light of the peasant." A great piece of writing and one often published in collections of the world's best short-stories is his sketch called "The Father."

Bjørnson is Norway's greatest lyric poet. He wrote the national song, "Yes, We Love This Land of Ours." He wrote other songs that are equally loved by Norwegians and known by heart. A friend once asked him upon what occasion he had felt most fully the joy of being a poet. He said:

"It was when a party from the Right in Christiania came to my house and smashed all my windows. For, when they had finished their assault and were starting home again, they felt that they must sing something, and consequently began to sing, 'Yes, We Love This Land of Ours.' They couldn't help themselves; they had to sing the song of the man they had attacked."

Bjørnson was active in politics as a robust reformer. He vied with Ibsen in problem plays and preached regeneration with as searching an intensity. Bjørnson wrote fourteen such plays, which mark the second period of his leadership of his people. "The King" is thought by many to be his greatest dramatic composition with a modern message. It should be read today in view of the titanic European struggle.

"In God's Ways" is one of Bjørnson's great novels, and has been looked upon as a summary of his philosophy.

WILLIAM ALLINGHAM (1828-1889)

We do not think of William Allingham as an editor of a magazine, though he was, of *Fraser's*, for many years. We do not think of him as a member of a literary circle, although he was, of one that included Ruskin, Carlyle, and Tennyson. We do not think of Allingham as a critic of his times and a friend of the pre-Raphaelites, though he was both, and warmly admitted by them to their councils. We do not think of him as intellectually like Dante Gabriel Rossetti or William Morris, though, like them, he was intellectually of other streets than the streets of London.

Much less do we think of William Allingham as an Irish coast officer of customs, or a clerk in a bank. Though he was all these identities in turn, rising step by step gradually through his own worth and efforts from the time when as a boy of fourteen he entered his father's employ, unschooled, and began mastering Greek, Latin, German, and French alone, we do not think of him as these. We think of him merely as a wraith of song. He set himself free with his own words—all those written long before, and those written some time before, and read, when his body, according to his wish, was cremated in 1889:

> Body to purifying flame,
> Soul to the Great Deep whence it came,
> Leaving a song on earth below,
> An urn of ashes white as snow.

What he did for children. No one has written a better child's song than Allingham's *Fairy Folk* or than *Robin Redbreast*. No one has sung better of ruined chapels, or winter pears, or bubbles. No one has shown a lighter touch or more aerial fancy. *Fairy Folk* has in it the quintessence of the subject. It is true to the Irish conception of the fairies, moreover, suggesting the fear and the attraction they inspire. Three indelible pictures are drawn in three dainty stanzas, framed in repetition. The repetition is itself inspiriting and is a true song device.

How he did it. If we think of the singer at all and not only of his poems, we think of him in his early manhood, going— even then like a wraith—up and down, unrecognized, in front of cottage doors where Irish girls sat singing. We think of his listening, of his taking bits out of the mouths of the singers, and hurrying home and finishing a ballad in his own way, and bringing or sending it back on a long strip of blue paper like an old song, and then coming again and hearing it sung unconsciously as an ancient ballad by the same Irish girls sitting singing in the same doorways.

Or we like best to think of him as he liked to think of himself

114

as a small Irish boy at home in an out-of-the-way little town on the extreme edge of Europe—in Ballyshannon, County Donegal, Ireland. He has said in one of his letters that he loved to sit in the tiny room in the roof where the tree branches met across the window and he could look down through them into the garden with flowers below. A little town Ballyshannon was, in his memory, with a river running to the sea, and a tide, and a lake with islands, blue mountains in the distance, trees, boulders, windy pastures, clouds, and America to the west!

THE FOLK TALES OF *SECOND READER*

Boots and his Brothers. Boots is just such a saga hero as is the lad who went to the north wind's house. He is unafraid and inquisitive. He wants to know the why of everything. Because he persists good-naturedly in spite of taunts, he finds out. This is an excellent lesson for the schoolroom, but teachers should not, of course, fall into the habit of preaching and of using every story for a sermon. Stories were invented to relieve us from preaching. The "moral" of this tale needs no emphasis. An interesting parallel could be drawn between Boots and Mr. Edison. The marvels attendant upon the inquiries of the one are not so great as the marvels attendant upon the inquiries of the other. For Mr. Edison, not only do axes hew and hack and spades dig and delve without man's muscles being immediately applied, but absent persons talk and sing as if present.

The Elves and the Shoemaker is a typical folk fairy tale. It is one of a group published by Grimm under the title "The Elves" (39). It is called "The First Story." The others are called "The Second Story" and "The Third Story." The second is about a servant girl who has a sort of Rip Van Winkle experience with the elves; and the third is about a changeling. Grimm's versions come from Hesse, but in the notes he mentions a number of variants. Such tales are numerous in the south of Scotland and the north of England. Grimm directs attention to a peculiar feature of elf personality. The little creatures disappear, he says, if clothes are given to them. A little sea-dwarf will have none of them, and vanishes when he receives them; a fairy man is given a little red coat, is delighted with it, but disappears. The cauld lad of Hilton, who set himself to determine the good qualities of the servants of Hilton castle, by his tricks and his ways, was himself undone at length through a little green cloak and hood which were laid out for him. He seized them in delight.

> "Here's a cloak and there's a hood,
> And the cauld lad of Hilton will do no more good,"

said he, and disappeared forever. Milton has enshrined the "lubber-fiend" of the kitchen hearth in L'Allegro.

These stories are fairy tales as distinct from nursery sagas. In these the fairies are the protagonists.

Cinderella. Three hundred and forty-five variants of Cinderella have been found. They are tabulated and discussed in a ponderous volume published by the Folklore Society of London over the signature of Marion Roalfe Cox, with an introduction by Andrew Lang. It is needless to say that the story is an important one and seems to have hanging to its skirts almost every other folk tale of the ages. We cannot here trace the variations, nor do we wish to. We will note only the fact that the version given in the school readers derives from Perrault and not from Grimm. The distinctive marks of Perrault are the fairy godmother, the pumpkin, the mice, the rat, the lizards, and the little slipper of glass; also the admonition to leave the ball at twelve o'clock, and the forgiveness of the haughty sisters by the gentle Cinderella. Grimm's version is much more primitive, much more of the common people. The neglected little girl weeps over her mother's grave and plants a hazel branch on it, which grows into a tree. From this tree drop down the fine clothes and the slippers embroidered in silk and silver, The German Cinderella does not forgive her sisters, who cut off portions of their feet in trying to prove that they can wear the slipper. Instead of finding forgiveness or success, they have their perfidy revealed and have their eyes plucked out by the pigeons that live in the branches of the hazel tree.

Other versions are still more harsh. Andrew Lang tells us that the Italian Cinderella breaks her stepmother's neck with the lid of a chest.

Perrault's good taste in the promotion of the story is evident. Some antiquarians would find fault with him for bringing the narrative to the drawing-room. One's reply can only be that Perrault was not an antiquarian, and that there are drawing-rooms as well as sculleries. It would seem a pity if so good a story should be lost to either place. A further promotion of the narrative is evident in our version. Here the stepmother is lacking. Perrault retained her as a natural folk explanation of the difference in temperament between the sisters and Cinderella. It is a question how far the refinement can go and still leave the central vitality: but it is certain that so long a story lives as everybody's property, as a folk tale transmitted orally for the larger part of its existence, it will change, antiquarians and recorders notwithstanding.

Hans in Luck is an excellent droll, one of the best of its kind. Grimm took it from Wernicke, who took it from oral tradition. Grimm follows it with the story of *Hans Married*, which ends in a direct joke. *Hans Married*, like the stories of Clever Hans, Clever Elsie, and Gambling Hansel, is not so wholesome and does not show so light a touch as does *Hans in Luck*.

The Queen Bee. The youngest brother in the story of *The Queen Bee* is Boots again, without Dasent's name for him. His attitude is the same towards nature wherever we find him. Simple faith and thoughtful brotherliness are good traits. They always call out help. The incident of the old man and the stone table with its inscription looks like an importation from the *Arabian Nights*. The bee-and-the-honey idea is also oriental in its ingenuousness.

The Sister of the Sun and The Flying Ship. Lars of the Lapland folk tale and Ivan of the Russian are both true nursery saga heroes. They are of humble birth. Lars is the son of a gardener and Ivan of a poor couple. They both lived near the palace. They both go on adventures to secure prizes to be brought to the rulers, and each wins a princess to wife after hazardous tasks are performed. Both stories, too, have a myth atmosphere, ample and suggestive. The golden hen that belongs to the Sister of the Sun offers the adherents of the Aryan theory much opportunity for discussion; as well as the fox's blowing out of the candles with the coming of night; the escape of Lars and Princess Sunset over the mountains; the arrival at the castle of Princess Sunrise.

Our schoolchildren may remember that Lapland is the country of the Northern Lights. Many little boys and girls up there must have asked questions about that beautiful phenomenon. Some small second-grade pupil in an American classroom might for the pleasure of composition answer them, making up a fanciful explanation in a story starting with the characters in this narrative of *The Sister of the Sun;* Lars, Princess Sunrise, Princess Sunset, the fox with the great yellow brush of a tail, the golden hens, the giants in their black shadow castle, the little prince, also, left along with his bow and arrows—What did he do?

Where the Lapland story is curtailed the Russian is expanded. Ivan soon attains the flying ship, but his adventures with it and the tasks appointed him when he tries to turn it over to the king, are added. Swift Foot, Sharp Ear, Gobbler, Drinker, and Sure Shot are very likable, clumsy, old giants. The *skazki,* as the Russian folk tales are called in their own country, are fresher, more naïve and brilliant than the German. The reason may be that the whole Russian peasantry today is nearer the folk tale way of thinking than is the peasantry of any other northern country producing literature. The good old uncles with the magic straw and the magic wood seem as familiar to us as our own aged Man in the Moon. Today, certainly, the Czar has his flying ship, and Sure Shot and the man with the magic wood must ride in it.

Why the Sea is Salt is a folk myth, by definition, since it accounts in a fanciful way for a natural phenomenon. The elements of the tale are myth elements historically, also, coming down in the lays of the Poetic *Edda* and in Snorri's Prose *Edda*. The story is told also by Saxo Grammaticus, the Danish "historian," who wrote in Latin in the twelfth and thirteenth centuries. *Grottasongr* (lay of Grotti) is the lay of the magic mill that would grind out anything one wished. The mill belonged to Frodi, a beneficent king, who ground only peace and plenty. Gold, Frodi's meal, lay about on the highway and in the field unsown. In Snorri's *Skaldskaparmal* the tale is finished. One day Frodi got from the King of Sweden two giant handmaidens, Fenja and Menja, whom he set to grind the mill. These he gave no rest, compelling them night and day to turn out peace and plenty for his realm; but Frodi had forgotten the nature of the mill, which was to grind what the grinder chose. Now the maidens' hearts had become hot and revengeful. They wished for fire and war. That very night King Mysing the skipper, the sea-rover, Frodi's enemy, came and slew him and seized the maidens and the mill. Mysing, too, was a tyrant towards the maidens. He bade them grind salt. When they wished to stop, he bade them grind on. They ground fast and furiously until the ship sank with them and their tyrant and the mill to the bottom of the ocean.

The homeliness of folk thinking is displayed in the modifications of the story as it went its rounds among the common people orally. Asbjørnsen and Moe brought it back into written literature in their collection. Other very ancient myth elements are evident in the story. The people who live down below and want for meat represent old ideas about the place that Asbjørnsen and Moe, following the popular vocabulary and mythology, frankly call Hell. To the Norsemen originally Hel was a giant goddess, mistress of nine worlds. She had charge of all those who died unfortunately and not in battle. A bitter cold place hers was, where firewood was needed. Well might the old man with the long white beard stand chopping at the gate.

Inconsistencies in an old story are often explainable by traditions contemporary with the growth of the narrative or antecedent to it. Take the question that some wide-awake boy might ask concerning this tale. If the old mill would grind anything the owner wished, why did not the people who live down below grind out a flitch of bacon rather than demand it of the visitor? And why in the first place were they so anxious for meat? A Norseman in the old days would understand these allusions. In the Halls of the Goddess Hel meat was scarce. The

119

greatest comforts of life were there forbidden, and what more nearly the greatest comfort in a cold country than meat? The general taboo of the place would counteract the particular virtue of the mill.

The Sleeping Beauty. Andrew Lang thinks it useless to try to interpret *The Sleeping Beauty* throughout as a nature myth, though he admits that the idea of the long sleep may have been derived from the repose of nature in winter. He notices how the story is a patchwork of incidents recurring elsewhere in different combinations. There is an ancient Egyptian narrative with a very similar beginning. The quarrel of the fairies (or the Wise Women, Grimm calls them) is the old discord at the wedding of Peleus, told in folk style. The maiden's sleep and her rescue are, as Grimm boldly asserts and Lang agrees, the wooing of Brunhild by Sigurd from the old Norse saga. The incident of the prick of the spindle has many analogies. Grimm says that the spindle is the sleep-thorn with which Odin pierces Brunhild. Lang calls attention to the poisoned nail and the poisoned comb in other sleep narratives.

The version of the story given in *Second Reader* is Grimm's *Little Briar Rose* with Perrault's title and fairies. The Italian version (in the *Pentamarone*) and the French version (*La Belle au Bois Dormant*) are each longer and less pleasant.

One of the old Eddaic lays called *Svipdag and Menglod* has elements of both the Cinderella and Sleeping Beauty stories. The first part of the poem relates how Svipdag, who is in love with the beautiful Menglod, visits the grave of his dead mother Groa and asks for help (Cinderella). Menglod is guarded in a strong castle (Sleeping Beauty) and is to be married to no one but her destined lover. Svipdag (Day Spring) turns out to be that lover.

Burne-Jones did a series of paintings illustrating *Briar Rose*.

East o' the Sun and West o' the Moon is one of the most charming folk tales that have come down to us. The title itself is inviting. One could never pass it by without taking up the story. William Morris has turned it into verse in *The Earthly Paradise*. It is already poetry in its suggestiveness in

Asbjørnsen and Moe's collection. Nor is the poetry lost in our version, which is derived from Dasent's translation. For obvious reasons, a number of the incidents are omitted in the reader, but the spirit and flavor of the diction remain, as well as the delightful stimulus of the personification. The trolls are true Norse *dramatis personae* of folk stories. Bursting is their usual and thrilling exit.

Hansel and Gretel. The little drama of *Hansel and Gretel* is adapted from a German opera in three acts, the libretto of which was written by Adelheid Wette and the music by Englebert Humperdinck (Wette's brother, a German composer, 1854-1921). The piece has the subtitle "A Fairy Opera," justified by the fact that the Sandman and the Dewman bear also the appellations of Sleep Fairy and Dawn Fairy. The characters appearing are the same as in the adaptation, except that the fourteen angels are materialized. Since they are totaled in the prayer situation in full number, some American small boy in counting up their detailed work may discover that two have escaped the adapters, unless 6 x 2 = 14.

The opera is of the last century, but the story on which it is founded is ancient and widespread. There are variants in all German dialects and in Italian and French. Maeterlinck's *Blue Bird* will occur to everyone familiar with modern drama. The allegorical signification is a philosopher's addition. Grimm tells the story in the Hesse version under the title of *Hansel and Gretel.* A white bird sits on a bough and sings a beautiful song, which arrests the children. They follow the singer until it alights on the roof of a house built of bread and covered with cakes and fitted with windows of clear sugar. Events follow as in the drama but with other incidents prefixed and added.

The beginning of the narrative is the world-old *motif* of the attempt of a stepmother to be rid of the expense and annoyance of her stepchildren. Refine the idea as we will, ignore it as we may in these cultivated times, it is yet founded on true psychology. Primitive man everywhere recognized the process of thought and recorded it in his crude way in many stories.

The adaptation of the opera is very spirited and wholesome. Any child would enjoy it.

CPSIA information can be obtained
at www.ICGtesting.com
Printed in the USA
FFOW02n0411140618
47104992-49566FF